W9-CYS-783

FRUIT OF THE SPIRIT

Pulse

track: discipleship

Gregg Farah
general editor
Kara Eckmann Powell

God's word for a jr. high world

Gospel Light

Gospel Light is an evangelical Christian publisher dedicated to serving the local church. We believe God's vision for Gospel Light is to provide church leaders with biblical, user-friendly materials that will help them evangelize, disciple and minister to children, youth and families.

It is our prayer that this Gospel Light resource will help you discover biblical truth for your own life and help you minister to youth. May God richly bless you.

For a free catalog of resources from Gospel Light, please contact your Christian supplier or contact us at 1-800-4-GOSPEL *or* www.gospellight.com.

PUBLISHING STAFF
William T. Greig, Publisher
Dr. Elmer L. Towns, Senior Consulting Publisher
Pam Weston, Editor
Patti Pennington Virtue, Assistant Editor
Christi Goeser, Editorial Assistant
Kyle Duncan, Associate Publisher
Bayard Taylor, M.Div., Senior Editor, Biblical and Theological Issues
Dr. Gary S. Greig, Senior Advisor, Biblical and Theological Issues
Kevin Parks, Cover Designer
Rosanne Richardson, Cover Production
Debi Thayer, Designer
Siv Ricketts and Donna Fitzpatrick, Contributing Writers

ISBN 0-8307-2547-4
© 2000 by Gospel Light
All rights reserved.
Printed in the U.S.A.

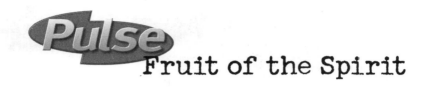

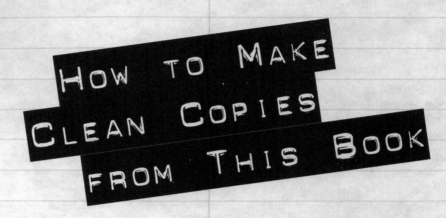

You may make copies of portions of this book with a clean conscience if:

- you (or someone in your organization) are the original purchaser;
- you are using the copies you make for a noncommercial purpose (such as teaching or promoting your ministry) within your church or organization;
- you follow the instructions provided in this book.

However, it is ILLEGAL for you to make copies if:

- you are using the material to promote, advertise or sell a product or service other than for ministry fund-raising;
- you are using the material in or on a product for sale;
- you or your organization are **not** the original purchaser of this book.

By following these guidelines you help us keep our products affordable.

Thank you,

Gospel Light

*Pages with the following notation can be legally reproduced:

There is a cry from this generation for Truth. **Pulse** curriculum targets this cry by leading teenagers to the Truth. How exciting it is to have a curriculum that gives the depth through Scripture and fun through involvement. —**Helen Musick**, Youth Specialties National Resource Team member, national speaker and author

The **Pulse** curriculum is truly "cross-cultural." Built on the solid foundation of an understanding of junior highers' unique developmental needs and rapidly changing culture, it affords teachers and youth workers the opportunity to communicate God's unchanging Word to kids growing up in a world that increasingly muffles and muddles the truth. —**Walt Mueller**, President, Center for Parent/Youth Understanding and author of *Understanding Today's Youth Culture*

The creators and writers of this curriculum know and love young teens, and that's what sets good junior high curriculum apart from the mediocre stuff! —**Mark Oestreicher,** Vice President of Ministry Resources, Youth Specialties

Great biblical material, creative interaction and USER-FRIENDLY! What more could you ask? This stuff will help you see your junior highers reach their potential as disciples of Christ! I highly recommend it! —**Ken Davis**, President, Dynamic Communications International and award-winning author and speaker

It's about time that curriculum produced for junior highers took them and their youth workers seriously. **Pulse** does it and does it very well! This curriculum knows junior highers and proves that teens changed by Christ who are equipped and empowered by His Church really can change their world! I am planning to recommend **Pulse** enthusiastically to all my youth worker friends. —**Rich Van Pelt,** Strategic Relationships Director, Compassion International, author, speaker and veteran youth worker

I found **Pulse** to be a stimulating, engaging and spiritually challenging curriculum for middle school students. Kara Powell has developed a rich resource that provides teachers with strong content to teach and creative options to help teachers meet the individual needs of their students. Recognizing that spiritual formation is not an end in itself, **Pulse** provides a strategy for evangelism in each lesson that empowers students to share the gospel with their peers. This is a curriculum that makes genuine connections with middle school students and the culture in which they must live out their faith every day. —**Mark W. Cannister, Ed.D.,** Chair, Department of Youth Ministries, Gordon College

Written by veteran junior high youth workers who know how to communicate so kids will get the message! Kara has given youth workers a fresh tool that's user-friendly and geared to make a lasting impact by addressing the foundational issues of Christianity that sometimes take a backseat to trendy topical studies. —**Paul Fleischmann**, Executive Director, National Network of Youth Ministries

This is serious curriculum for junior highers! Not only does it take the great themes of the Christian faith seriously, but it takes junior highers seriously, as well. Young adolescents have a tremendous capacity for learning about spiritual things and this curriculum makes it possible for them to learn all they can about the God of the Bible—who loves them and wants to involve them *now* in His Church. This is the best I've seen yet. —**Wayne Rice**, author and Junior High Ministry Director, Understanding Your Teenager seminars

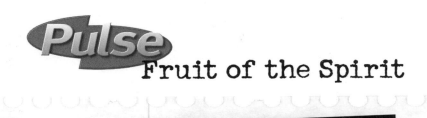

Fruit of the Spirit

CONTENTSCONTENTSCONTENTSCONTENTSCONTENTS

2005–2006

Unit I: Fruit for Ourselves

Unit II: Fruit for Others

Sep
Jan
Feb

Love

kindness

Goodness

missing pp 81–??

Dedication

To God, may my life
and the lives of
those who use this
curriculum bear fruit
so that You are hon-
ored and many would
follow You.

...You've Made the Right Choice in Choosing Pulse for Your Junior Highers

The Top Ten Reasons...

9. Junior highers need and deserve youth workers who are expert trainers and teachers of biblical truth.

   Every book is pulsating with youth leader tips and a full-length youth worker article designed to infuse YOU with more passion and skill for your ministry to junior highers.

10. Junior highers equate who God is with what church is like. To them a boring youth ministry means a boring God.

    Fun and variety are the twin threads that weave their way through this curriculum's every page.

8. Junior highers need ongoing reminders of the big idea of each session.

   Wouldn't it be great if you could give your students devotionals every week to reinforce the learning goals of the session? Get this: YOU CAN because THIS CURRICULUM DOES.

7. Some of our world's most effective evangelists are junior highers.

   Every session, and we mean EVERY session, concludes with an evangelism option that ties "the big idea" of the session to the big need to share Christ with others.

6. Since no two junior highers (or their leaders) look, think or act alike, no two junior high ministries look, think or act alike.

   Each step comes with three options that you can cut and paste to create a session that works best for YOUR students and YOUR personality.

5. Junior highers' growing minds are ready for more than just fun and games with a little Scripture thrown in.

   Scripture is the very skeleton of each session, giving it its shape, its form and its very life.

4. Junior highers learn best when they can see, taste, feel and experience the session.

   This curriculum involves students in every step through active learning and games to prove to students that following Christ is the greatest adventure ever.

3. Tragically, most junior highers are under challenged in their walks with Christ.

   We've packed the final step of each session with three options that serve to move students a few steps forward in their walks with Christ.

2. Junior highers tend to understand the Bible in bits and pieces and miss the big picture of all that God has done for them.

   This curriculum follows a strategic three-year plan that walks junior highers through the Bible, stopping at the most important points along the way.

1. Junior highers are moving through all sorts of changes—from getting a new body to getting a new locker.

   We've designed a curriculum that revolves around one simple vision: moving God's Word into a junior high world.

Moving Through Pulse

Since **Pulse** is vibrating with so many different learning activities, this guide will help you pick and choose the best possible options for *your* students.

THE SESSIONS

The six sessions are split into two stand-alone units, so you can choose to teach either three or six sessions at a time. Each session is geared to be 45 to 90 minutes long and is comprised of the following four steps.

IT'S YOUR MOVE

A training article for you, the youth worker, to show you *why* and *how* to see students' worlds changed by Christ to change the world.

STEP 1 — MOVING IN

This first step helps students focus in on the theme of the lesson in a fun and engaging way through three options:

 MOVE IT—An active learning experience that may or may not involve all of your students.

 CHAT ROOM—Provocative, clear and simple questions to get your students thinking and chatting.

 FUN AND GAMES—Zany, creative and competitive games that may or may not involve all of your students.

STEP 2 — MOVING UP

The second step enables students to look up to God by relating the very words of Scripture to the session topic through three options:

 MOVE IT—An active learning experience that may or may not involve all of your students.

 CHAT ROOM—Provocative, clear and simple questions to get your students chatting about the Scripture lesson.

 **PULSE POINTS**—A message outline with simple points and meaningful illustrations to give students some massive truths about Scripture with hardly any preparation on your part.

STEP 3
MOVING ON

STEP 4
MOVING OUT

This step asks students to look inward and discover how God's Word connects with their own worlds through three options:

 CHAT ROOM—Provocative, clear and simple questions to get your students chatting.

 REAL LIFE—A case study about someone (usually a junior higher) who needs your students' help figuring out what to do.

 TOUGH QUESTIONS—Four to six mind-stretching questions that challenge students to a new level of depth and integration.

This final step leads students out into their world with specific challenges to apply at school, at home and with their friends through three options based on your students' growth potential:

 LIGHT THE FIRE—For junior highers who may or may not be Christians and need easily accessible application ideas.

 **FIRED UP**—For students who are definitely Christians and are ready for more intense application ideas.

 SPREAD THE FIRE—A special evangelism application idea for students with a passion to see others come to know Christ.

OTHER IMPORTANT MOVING PARTS

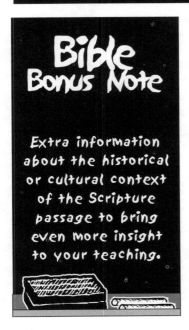

Bible Bonus Note

Extra information about the historical or cultural context of the Scripture passage to bring even more insight to your teaching.

Youth Leader Tip

Suggestions, options and/or other useful information to make your life easier or at least more interesting!

Devotions in Motion

WEEK FIVE: GRACE

Four devoTionals for each session To keep The big idea moving Through your junior highers' lives all week long.

ON THE MOVE—An appealing, easy-to-read handout you can give your junior highers to help them learn how to understand the necessity of prayer in their lives and how it will help them to culitvate a personal relationship with God.

Do You Have the Fruit?

It's Your Move

Fruit Happens. Maybe you've seen that phrase on a bumper sticker or sign at a Christian bookstore. *Fruit Happens.* In other words, once you become a Christian, you will inevitably start to change and demonstrate some of that juicy fruit of the Spirit. But wait a minute. How inevitable is it—really?

Perhaps a better bumper sticker would be: *Fruit happens if you try.* Maybe you're a more saintly youth leader than I am, but I find that developing love, joy, peace, patience, kindness, goodness, faithfulness, gentleness and self-control doesn't always come naturally. I have to work at it. First, I have to ask for God's grace to strengthen me as I make choices every day. Then I have to make those choices, deciding whether or not to vent my frustration at the grocery store clerk for the long checkout line, how frustrated I should be with the eighth grade boy who punches a hole in our youth room wall, and what I say on the phone to a mom who blames me for the problems her daughter is causing at home.

These kinds of choices are also being thrown rapid-fire at your junior highers. How will they respond when their parents ask them to baby-sit a younger brother? What will they do when their friends are making fun of the new kid sitting by herself in the lunch court? When the pressures of homework, soccer and piano practices get stressful, how will your students react?

Without God's grace, a series of courageous decisions and the support of a caring community, it's tough to say. But with God, a little bit of boldness and your support, the odds of junior highers responding in a fruity way get a little better.

We've strategically designed this book to equip students with the knowledge and skills they need to demonstrate the fruit of the Spirit.

Every lesson is based not just on a specific fruit but also on a specific story that highlights what this fruit looks like in action.

For junior highers, principles speak pages, but stories speak volumes. Every lesson is founded upon an example from the gospel of someone who did, or maybe didn't, know how to live out that specific fruit. That means no more guessing about what that fruit looks like in real life.

Every lesson revolves around Christ and His role in developing fruit in our lives.

What makes this curriculum different from lessons about character that might be taught at the local YMCA or Jewish Community Center is the centrality of Christ. Every story involves Him, and every lesson reminds students of the difficulty of trying to live the Christian life apart from a dynamic, ongoing relationship with Christ.

Every lesson helps students contextualize the fruit in a language and setting that makes sense to them.

Each lesson transports students into real-life school scenarios and everyday interactions with their friends. Then they get to wrestle with how to translate what the Bible teaches into their own worlds. It's not always easy, but prayerfully, by the end of each lesson, they'll be able to pin it down.

Kara Eckmann Powell

Contributors

Siv Ricketts, author of the student devotionals, is a student ministries director, freelance writer and editor living in San Diego, California. Siv and her husband, Dave, have been ministering to students together for the past six years and have recently been blessed with a new son, Corban.

Donna Fitzpatrick, author of the student article "How Do I Pray?" lives in Northern California with her husband, Dan, and seven of her eight children. With the oldest in her third year of college and the youngest in her third year of age, life is never dull! Donna enjoys writing, public speaking and homeschooling.

 Fruit of the Spirit

The Big Idea

True self-control is being obedient to God's will when we are tempted by our own desires.

Session Aims

In this session you will guide students to:

- Understand the value of exercising self-control;
- Be thankful for God's plan to help them live healthy lives;
- Commit to avoiding a sin they struggle with this week.

The Biggest Verse

Self-Control

"Jesus answered, 'It is written: "Man does not live on bread alone, but on every word that comes from the mouth of God."'" Matthew 4:4

Other Important Verses

Psalm 91; 119:9-11; Proverbs 6:27; Matthew 4:1-11; 7:7-10; 1 Corinthians 10:13,14; Galatians 5:22-24; Philippians 4:13; 2 Peter 1:5-8

STEP 1 — MOVING IN

This step helps students realize that we all struggle with showing self-control.

Option 1 — Move It

You'll need Zee book, zee book!

Greet students and have everyone stand facing front and inform them that you're going to play a game of Simon Says. (Go ahead and use your own name—Simon won't mind.) Ask for a show of hands for those who've played this game before. Anyone raising his or her hand is outta there—Simon didn't say! OK, OK, let them back into the game. To insure they can see you, ask them to move closer to the front. You guessed it—whoever moves closer to the front is out again!

While you have a captive audience, have a brief discussion on what self-control is and invite students (Simon says) to give examples of what it means to show self-control. After a couple of minutes of discussion, play on!

Play a couple of rounds if you have time; then transition to the next step by explaining: **This game proves that even when we try to show self-control, it can be tough! We all struggle with this—except for the winner of our game today**. Offer a congratulatory handshake. Oops! If the winner shakes, he or she is *out*—Simon didn't say! **Self-control is just the first of a series of qualities called the "fruit of the Spirit." As we'll see today, even Jesus had to decide what it meant to show self-control.**

Option 2 — Chat Room

You'll need A table, a pillowcase, an old trophy, a tasty dessert (brownies, cookies, candy, etc.), a folded note that clearly says "PERSONAL!" and a box with an easy to open lid. **High-tech option:** If you can pull it off, have a hidden video camera pointed right at the table and show

the results during the discussion. **Low-tech option:** Arrange for an older, trustworthy student to visit the session and let her in on the gag. She can watch the action from inside the room without anyone thinking twice about her presence.

Ahead of time, place the table at the front of the room and arrange for two adult volunteers to carry in the items listed and place them on the table when you give the signal. They should make sure the trophy is covered with the pillowcase and the dessert remains uncovered.

After students arrive, ask them to take a seat and welcome them to this session—that will be the signal for the items to be brought in. At this point, act very excited about what's under the pillowcase and what's inside the box and make a big deal about the dessert (how tasty it looks, etc.). Let students know that you need to have a quick meeting and you'll be back in about five minutes. Leave the room with the adults and on your way out, have one of the volunteers casually drop the note marked "PERSONAL!" on the floor. Be sure that an adult can observe how students are reacting to the temptations in the room. After three minutes or so, come back into the room and discuss:

Did anyone struggle with the temptation of reading the note? Remind students that you're asking if anyone *struggled* with the temptation, not if anyone acted on the temptation. Most of the students will admit to struggling with it.

What made it difficult? No one was looking; it might have been something really interesting.

Did anyone struggle with the temptation of looking under the pillowcase? Probably. Again, you're asking if anyone *struggled* with the temptation itself.

What about the temptation of looking in the box?

What about the temptation of just taking a *teeny tiny* piece of dessert?

Was one of the temptations stronger than the others? Why or why not?

Who *wasn't* tempted? Check the pulse of anyone not raising his or her hand!

What made it easier for you? Afraid of getting caught; knowing it was wrong; not wanting to ruin a surprise.

What are some temptations that junior highers struggle with? Smoking, drugs, cheating on tests, skipping class, etc.

Who struggles sometimes with showing self-control? Assuming that all of the students are human, all of their hands should be in the air (and yours, too!).

Ask volunteers to distribute the dessert. Transition to the next step by explaining: **None of us is tempted by the same things, but every one of us is tempted. And we all struggle with self-control at different times. Self-control is just the first of a series of qualities called the "fruit of the Spirit." As we'll see today, even Jesus had to decide what it meant to show self-control.**

Option 3  Fun and Games

You'll need Some earplugs are a good idea, but not necessary. This can get noisy!

Greet students and divide them into small groups of five or six; then instruct each group to sit in a circle. Ask for a show of hands of students who think they have pretty good self-control; then challenge groups with the following test:

One at a time, each person in a group must name a rule for the group and a consequence for breaking that rule. The rule should be one that's easily broken (for example, no sentences can start with a vowel; everyone must keep their hands away from their bodies at all times; when speaking, a person must look directly into the eyes of the person on his or her right, regardless of who he or she is actually speaking to). The consequence can be zany and fun (for example, running around another group's circle while singing "Happy Birthday;" kissing the feet of any adult in the room; hugging someone in another group and telling him or her how wonderful he or she is).

Give the signal and allow several minutes for students to walk around and talk to each other while trying not to break any rules. Transition to the next step by explaining: **We all struggle with showing self-control. Sometimes the consequences are insignificant, but other times they can be costly. Self-control is just the first of a series of qualities called the "fruit of the Spirit." As we'll see today, even Jesus had to decide what it meant to show self-control.**

STEP 2 MOVING UP

This step shows students that the Bible helps them respond to every temptation that life can offer.

Option 1  Move It

You'll need Your Bible, a white board, a dry-erase marker, paper and pens or pencils.
Ahead of time, write the following group numbers and Scripture references on the white board: Group 1—Matthew 4:1-4; Group 2—Matthew 4:5-7; Group 3—Matthew 4:8-11; then write "What would Satan tempt Jesus with today that is similar to this?" at the bottom of the white board.

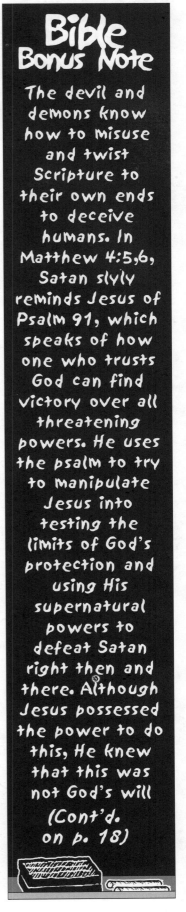

Bible Bonus Note

The devil and demons know how to misuse and twist Scripture to their own ends to deceive humans. In Matthew 4:5,6, Satan slyly reminds Jesus of Psalm 91, which speaks of how one who trusts God can find victory over all threatening powers. He uses the psalm to try to manipulate Jesus into testing the limits of God's protection and using His supernatural powers to defeat Satan right then and there. Although Jesus possessed the power to do this, He knew that this was not God's will (Cont'd. on p. 18)

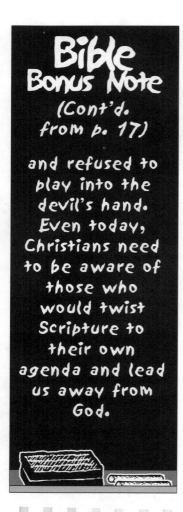

Bible Bonus Note

(Cont'd. from p. 17)

and refused to play into the devil's hand. Even today, Christians need to be aware of those who would twist Scripture to their own agenda and lead us away from God.

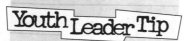

Youth Leader Tip

Here are two things you can do to make a public survey experience more enjoyable for you and your interviewees: (1) ask general questions first before asking specific ones, and (2) offer a "thank you" gift for the interviewee's time (like free cookies, candy, gift certificate for ice cream, etc.).

Divide students into groups of five or six and distribute Bibles, paper and pens or pencils. Assign each group a number and its corresponding passage. It's OK to use a passage more than once if you have more than three groups. Instruct groups to look up their assigned verses and brainstorm on the following: a one- or two-sentence summary of what the verses are about; a modern temptation to replace what Jesus was tempted with and how to act out the modern temptation. Allow several minutes for brainstorming; then have groups act out the modern temptations they came up with.

Allow for as many groups to participate as you have time for; then discuss:

What temptations did Jesus face? Hunger, testing God, worldly possessions and power.

How did He respond to each temptation? He cited Scripture.

What was Jesus' method for facing temptation? Turning to God's Word.

How would Jesus respond to any of the temptations from the dramas? He would turn to God's Word for help.

What temptations do junior highers face today? Smoking, drugs, cheating on tests, skipping class to hang out with friends, etc.

How can you respond to those temptations?

Clarify the meaning and significance of Matthew 4 by incorporating the following information into the discussion:

- When Satan said, "If you are the Son of God" (vv. 3,6), he wasn't *really* doubting Jesus' identity—He knew the truth. He wanted to remind Jesus who He was and what He was able to do.
- When Satan tempted Jesus to transform the stones into bread (see v. 3), Jesus refused, not because there's anything wrong with making bread, but because He knew it would be wrong to rely on his own miracle-working power rather than on God's provision.
- When Satan told Jesus to jump from the highest part of the temple (see v. 6), Jesus refused, not because He was afraid God would not save Him, but because He knew that it was wrong to manipulate God
- When Satan tempted Jesus a third time with worldly riches (see vv. 8,9), Jesus refused because He knew that only God is worthy of worship and that no worldly riches can begin to compare with the rewards our heavenly Father holds for us in heaven.

Option 2  Chat Room

You'll need Several Bibles, a TV, a VCR, a video camera and a blank video tape. **Low-tech option:** Use an audiotape recorder instead of a video camera.

Ahead of time, prepare a brief (five minutes or so) video of a variety of people responding to the following two questions: *What is a temptation that most people face?* and *How might a person show self-control over that temptation?*

Introduce the video, summarizing the questions you asked in the video and the places you went to interview people. After watching the video, discuss:

What are other temptations you can think of?

What's the toughest temptation you can think of?

What are some other ways a person can show self-control against those temptations?

Distribute Bibles and ask volunteers to read Matthew 4:1-11 in turn, each reading three or four verses at a time. Clarify the meaning and significance of the passage by incorporating the information from Option 1 as you discuss:

What was Jesus tempted to do? Make stones into bread, jump off the Temple to test God's love and worship Satan.

Why did the devil choose those temptations? They are basic to what tempts all humans: physical, emotional and spiritual needs and desires that we can choose to depend on God to meet, or depend on our own (or Satan's) ways to meet. These temptations also represent the lust of the flesh, desire for power and worship of idols/Satan.

What was Jesus' tactic to fight that temptation? He used Scripture to deflate Satan's deceptions.

What key phrase did Jesus use in every response to temptation? "It is written."

How did Jesus show self-control by responding the way He did? He focused on God's truth rather than his own needs or desires.

How do you think Jesus would respond to the temptations we heard in the video?

What does that say about how we should respond to temptation?

Option 3  Pulse Points

You'll need Several Bibles, a section of newspaper, small sticks for kindling, a book of matches or a lighter, a chair and two candy bars (one snack size and one regular size) per student.

Ahead of time, place the chair at the front of the meeting room; then crumple up the newspaper and set it to the side.

The Big Idea

God can give us self-control.

The Big Question

What do I need to remember in order to develop self-control?

1. Remember what tempts you.

Distribute Bibles; then ask for a brave volunteer to sit in the chair at the front of the room. Arrange the crumpled newspaper and kindling on his lap just as you might do to create a small campfire. Let the volunteer know that you're curious to see how long he will sit there with a burning fire in his lap. As you approach him, strike a match or light the lighter as though you are really going to light the fire. When the volunteer (hopefully) bolts off his seat (or until you've taken the illustration as far as you can *without lighting the fire*) ask a student to read Proverbs 6:27 aloud.

Discuss how foolish it would be to build a fire in your lap and never think about the possibility of getting burned. Distribute a snack-size candy bar to each student. Tell them they can eat the candy right now if they absolutely can't resist, but that you would prefer they wait until the end of the lesson. Add to the temptation by emphasizing the qualities of the candy and make it as enticing as possible. Point out how similar the verse you just read is to the difficulty of holding candy you love and not being able to eat it. It's better to stay as far away from temptation as possible.

2. Remember Jesus' example.

Read Matthew 4:4 to illustrate how Jesus responded to temptation. Explain: **Jesus was hungry—a lot hungrier than most of us have ever been. He knew, though, that more than His body needed physical food, He needed spiritual nourishment from God's Word.** Ask students how they might apply Jesus' example to the candy temptation.

3. Remember to ask God for help.

Ask a volunteer to read Matthew 7:7,8 and 1 Corinthians 10:13,14. Discuss some of the serious issues that junior highers might face and how the way to have the strength to resist the temptations of life can only be obtained through God's mercy and grace when we go to Him in prayer.

4. Remember that God's will is always in your best interest.

Read Matthew 7:9,10; then discuss how God always answers our prayers with our best interest in mind even when His answers to our prayers are totally different than what we want them to be. Distribute the larger candy bars to students who still have not eaten their snack-sized candy. Don't give into the temptation to give a new one to students who already ate their snack-sized ones *no matter how much they whine*! It will cheapen the illustration. Explain: **When we resist temptation, we receive the benefits of living according to the plan of the One who knows us and loves us the most. Only He knows what's ahead and all we have to do is trust Him. Can it get any better than that?**

STEP 3
MOVING ON

This step helps students understand the value of exercising self-control.

Option 1  Chat Room

You'll need One copy of "Here's What I Think" (p. 23) and a pen or pencil for every five to six students.

Divide students into groups of five or six; then distribute "Here's What I Think" and pens or pencils. Instruct groups to brainstorm how to complete *only* the first sentence. Have an adult volunteer walk around and check to make sure nothing inappropriate is written on the handout.

Have groups exchange papers and complete the second sentence based on the response of the previous group.

Continue having groups trade handouts until all of the sentences have been completed. Each time a sentence is to be completed, their response must be based on what was previously written. It's OK if a group ends up with its own handouts.

When you're done, have a volunteer from each group come up front and read their completed sentences. Then, ask students who originally came up with the scenario to share one thing they learned from the other groups' ideas.

Option 2  Real Life

You'll need Nothin' but your front teeth!

Read the following story and then have students turn to the two people on either side of them to discuss the following questions, or discuss them as a large group.

> **Last summer at camp, Steve and I made a commitment not to drink alcohol. We are both into sports and want to stay healthy and, since it's illegal for us to drink anyway, we didn't want to dishonor God or our families.**
>
> **When school started, Steve started hanging out with a different crowd. We still did stuff together, but not like last year. One time at a party I saw him sip something from a cup. I asked him what it was, but he ignored me. I knew it was alcohol though, because I could smell it and because he avoided me the rest of the night. Plus, everyone he was hanging out with told me they'd beat me up if I said anything. The next Monday at school, I asked him about our commitment at camp, but Steve just walked away. I don't get it. And now I'm wondering what to do.**

Discuss:

Why did Steve give in to temptation? Probably peer pressure.

What was the consequence of that? He went back on his commitment to honor God and his family—not to mention himself.

If you were Steve's friend, what would you do about the friendship? Pray for him to have the strength to recommit himself to honoring God and keep trying to reach out to him to let him know that you care.

If you were Steve's friend, would it be easier or more difficult to show self-control yourself around alcohol? It would depend on the situation and the temptations of peer pressure, etc.

20

Option 3 — Tough Questions

You'll need Your Bible and these questions.

1. **Why do I struggle with the same sins over and over again?** Some sins have become habits, and since it took time to develop the habits, it will take time to overcome them. An important step is to recognize the situations that cause the temptation to sin and avoid those situations if you can. If a situation is unavoidable, keep yourself focused on avoiding the temptation; and when you're tempted—pray! If you've asked God to forgive you and to control your life, then spend some time reading Galatians 5:22-24. Use that as a prayer, asking God to help you live the lifestyle those verses describe. Finally, be patient. Your Christian life is a journey. Take one step at a time.

2. **What are some ways I can learn self-control?** Psalm 119:9-11 is a great passage to remind us that we've got to know what God's guidelines are for healthy living. Once you understand this, you can continue to pray for God to help you and you can ask a friend or parent to pray with you too.

3. **Why do I feel like I'm the only one struggling with self-control?** You're not! First Corinthians 10:13,14 is a terrific reminder that tells us that we're not alone and that God is always ready to help!

4. **Are there really any benefits to practicing self-control?** *Tons!* Second Peter 1:5-8 explains that self-control leads to perseverance; perseverance to godliness; godliness to brotherly kindness; brotherly kindness to love—and that all these things work together to bring you into a closer relationship with Jesus Christ. It's a chain reaction that only gets better with practice!

NOTES

STEP 4 — MOVING OUT

This step proves that even though it's tough to do, students will benefit when they exercise self-control this week.

Option 1 — Light the Fire

You'll need Several felt-tip pens and a bunch of balloons (at least one per student).

Explain that it's not easy to show self-control. Discuss: **What are the benefits of exercising our self-control, even though it's difficult?** Knowing we've honored God and done the right thing. Staying out of trouble!

What role does God play in providing self-control?

Distribute pens and balloons. Instruct students to write the word "self-control" on the balloons *before* they blow them up. Then blow them up and tie them off. (**Option:** Let them decorate the balloons too. They probably will anyway!)

Point out what happens to the words on the balloons as they are blown up. Explain: **This is similar to how God can work in our lives to help us have more self-control: the more air that goes into the balloon, the larger the "self-control" gets—the more we allow God to fill our lives, the more self-control we'll have.**

Close in prayer by giving students an opportunity to ask God to come in and control their lives.

Option 2 — Fired Up

You'll need Several Bibles, copies of "Next Steps" (p. 24) and pens or pencils.

Distribute Bibles, "Next Steps" and pens or pencils. Allow five minutes for students to complete the handout; then invite anyone who is willing to share what he or she wrote. **Optional:** Have the adults in the room (including you) complete the handout and share your answers too.

Youth Leader Tip

Praying aloud in a group is hard! But it's also a great tool for building relationships and accountability. Praying together can make quite an impact on students' lives. Share lots of encouragement for them as they pray and model what you want them to do. Give them baby steps if they're a bit overwhelmed such as asking them to respond with one word descriptions or things to thank God for; then move on to sentence prayers. When you pray, keep it simple and conversational so that they aren't intimidated about choosing the right words.

Discuss what is shared; then divide students into groups of three or four and have them pray for one another, by name, that they would have the strength to take their next steps toward self-control during the upcoming week.

Option 3

Spread the Fire

You'll need Copies of "Temptation and Self-Control" (p. 25) and pens or pencils.

Explain: **Sharing about Jesus with our non-Christian friends doesn't mean we have to have it all together. In fact, they can often relate to us better when we talk about our struggles and how Jesus is helping us in the midst of them.**

Distribute "Temptation and Self-Control" and pens or pencils. Allow a couple of minutes for students to complete the handout; then pair them off to share what they've written. After pairs have shared, invite anyone who would like to share his or her story with the whole group to do so.

Ask students to think of both a Christian friend and a non-Christian friend who they would be willing to share with in the next week about how God is helping them to show self-control in tempting areas of their lives. Have them write the initials of those people in the top left-hand corner of their handouts.

Join the pairs into groups of four or six and have each group pray first for one another and then for the people they'd like to tell their stories to. If you have enough adult volunteers, you can ask them to join groups and help guide students through the prayers.

NOTES

Here's What I Think

One thing that people my age struggle with is . . .

In order to show self-control with that struggle, I would . . .

If that didn't work, I would . . .

One consequence of not showing self-control in that situation is . . .

One benefit of showing self-control in that situation is . . .

Next Steps

Where are you struggling? Where are you most tempted?

One area where I really need self-control is . . .

Where are you? What's going on? Is there a pattern?

I'm usually tempted when . . .

What are some consequences?

When I don't show self-control, I usually suffer by . . .

How does it feel to be victorious?

When I do show self-control in this area, I find that I . . .

Here are some things I can do the next time I feel tempted:

Call this friend _____

Read this Bible verse _____
(If you don't have a favorite verse yet, Philippians 4:13 or
1 Corinthians 10:13,14 is a good place to start!)

Go to this place _____

Pray and ask God . . .

Temptation and Self-Control

One temptation I struggle with is . . .

The negative effect of giving into this temptation is . . .

God helps me to resist this temptation by . . .

When I show self-control and make the right decision, I feel . . .

Devotions in Motion

WEEK ONE: SELF-CONTROL

DAY 1

QUICK QUESTIONS

Be disciplined and read Proverbs 25:28.

God Says

After school one day, you and some friends decide to check out the stores in the new mall. While in the candy store, you see one of your friends slip a candy bar into her jacket pocket. When she sees your startled expression she says, "C'mon. It's easy. No one will notice. Besides, everyone does it. Go ahead. I dare you." How do you respond?

☐ Shrug and pick up some taffy to shove in your pocket.

☐ Smile and say, "No, thanks. I'd rather pay for it."

☐ Shrug and walk away without saying anything.

☐ Report your friend to the store manager.

I Do

What would happen to a house whose walls were broken down? It certainly wouldn't be a great place to live, would it? Do you have certain friends that tend to influence you badly? How do you respond when they want you to do things you know are wrong? When do you most need self-control?

This week when you're tempted to give in to what you know God wouldn't want you to do, imagine a wall in your room falling down if you give in. If it happens more than once, the roof would cave in. That should help you to resist when you are tempted!

FOLD HERE

DAY 4

FAST FACTS

Find out about the Spirit God gave you in 2 Timothy 1:7.

God Says

Even though most of her friends would be going to Brad's party, Jen signed up for her church's upcoming service project. Her friends couldn't understand why Jen would choose weeding, washing cars, painting a house, cleaning bathrooms and generally getting dirty over a huge party where everyone was going to have a blast.

After the weekend, Jen's friends couldn't wait to give her all the details of Brad's party. They weren't expecting her response. "Y'know, I missed you guys a lot and I'm sure the party was great, but I'm not sorry I decided to skip it because I got to help people and do things I've never done before—things I never even thought I could do. The trip I took this weekend while you went to Brad's party changed my life!"

I Do

Self-control means choosing what God wants you to do, even when it means giving up something you'd like to do. It can be hard, but doing what God wants is always best. Try it! You won't be sorry.

27

FAST FACTS

Read Titus 2:11,12 To discover The relationship beTween salvation and self-conTrol.

God Says

Everyone described Gregg as wild. He Talked back To Teachers, made messes with sugar and ketchup packets at EasT Good resTaurants and was The life of The party with his friends. When Gregg first came To church, kids who knew him couldn'T believe it. When he reTurned week after week, They were shocked. Then Gregg did something ToTally ouTrageous, even for him—he meT Jesus.

Gregg's sTill wild, but now he's wild about God. InsTead of Talking back To Teachers, he volunteers answers in class. Instead of a mess, he Tries To leave places looking beTTer Than he found Them. Gregg's sTill The life of The party, but now The party sometimes Takes place at church.

I Do.

Knowing Jesus has To make a difference in The way you live. Being a ChrisTian means you won'T do some of The Things oThers at school do, but iT doesn'T mean you can'T have fun. In facT, you can have even more fun because you won'T have To worry abouT The negaTive consequences of your wrong acTions. Ask Jesus To help you live a more self-conTrolled life This week.

FOLD HERE

QUICK QUESTIONS

Find ouT how noT To sin in Psalm 119:11.

God Says

What would you do if....

• You could plainly see your friend's answers To The hisTory TesT you were Taking—The one you didn'T even boTher To sTudy for?

• Your parenTs wanTed you To spend The evening with Them insTead of wiTh your friends?

• Someone at school asked you why you go To church?

• You heard a juicy rumor Too good noT To pass on?

Read and sTudy God's Word and you'll know right away how The wanTs you To respond To all of These siTuaTions!

I Do.

How did Jesus' familiarity wiTh ScripTure help Him pracTice self-conTrol when He was TempTed in The deserT?

What does Jesus' example Teach you about how you can resisT TempTaTion?

Ask your parenTs or youTh pasTor for some key ScripTure passages and starT hiding Them in your heart Today. That means memorizing Them

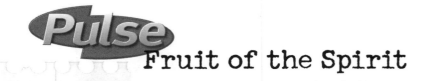

Fruit of the Spirit

The Big Idea

Real joy has nothing to do with circumstances; it comes only through knowing and obeying God.

Session Aims

In this session you will guide students to:

- Understand how to experience true joy, by knowing God *and* obeying Him;
- Be excited about their relationship with Christ;
- Choose to commit or recommit their lives to Christ today.

The Biggest Verse

"I have told you this so that my joy may be in you and that your joy may be complete." John 15:11

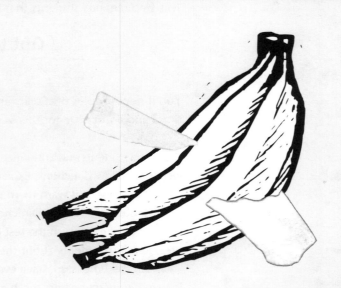

Joy

Other Important Verses

Psalm 80:8; Isaiah 5:1-7; 53:5; Ezekiel 15:1-8; Matthew 5:3-11; John 5:19,30; 10:10; 15:1-11; Romans 15:13; 1 Thessalonians 5:18; 1 Peter 2:24

STEP 1

MOVING IN

This step reminds students that there are benefits to obedience.

Option 1  Move It

You'll need Copies of "Following Directions" (p. 37), pens or pencils, a three-minute timer and a fun prize for the winner(s).

Welcome students and announce that you're going to give them a test to determine how well they follow directions. Explain that a prize will be given to those who get the most correct answers, but warn them that they only have three minutes to complete the test.

Distribute "Following Directions" to each student face down along with a pen or pencil. No one can turn the test over until you say "Begin." Set the timer to three minutes. Remind students about the time limit; then give the signal to begin.

When the time is up, have everyone stop and award the prize(s) to anyone who followed the directions on the handout. Transition to the next step by explaining: **It's important to follow the rules! Just as following the directions and being obedient made the difference on this test; the same is true in life. As we'll see today: when we obey God, we have the opportunity to experience true joy.**

Option 2  Chat Room

You'll need These questions.

Greet students and divide them into groups of four or five. Explain that you're going to have them respond to a variety of different questions; discussing their answers in their small groups. Ask the following questions one at a time and allow one to two minutes for small-group discussion between each question:

- **Would you rather get an *A* on a test that you cheated on *or* get a *C* on a test you did on your own?**
- **Would you rather obey your parents and come home on time *or* ignore curfew to meet your favorite celebrity?**
- **Would you rather save money for a year to buy something big *or* steal it and have it right away?**
- **Would you rather tell your parents you got in trouble at school *or* not tell them and hope they never find out?**
- **Would you rather obey your parents and wear the clothes they want you to wear *or* change into different clothes when you got to school?**
- **Would you rather see the movie you told your parents you would see *or* sneak into the R-rated movie everyone else has seen?**

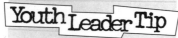

Youth Leader Tip

Encourage students to dig deeper in group discussions by using the following tips:
1. Always ask open-ended questions (ones that can't be answered with just yes or no).
2. Don't be afraid of silence (be willing to wait for a response to a question).
3. Be encouraging (remember that everyone needs positive reinforcement).

- Would you rather be friends with those who are faithful *or* with those who would make you popular?
- Would you rather tell the truth when answering all of these questions *or* lie about one or two?

When all the questions have been discussed, explain: **Obedience is always a choice. And sometimes not obeying seems appealing. Today we're going to look at whether or not obeying God is always the right thing and what the benefits of obedience are.**

Option 3  Fun and Games

You'll need A sturdy chair (you don't want to fall on your face in front of a bunch of junior highers!), some adult volunteers and a prize for the winner (and runners-up, if you want). **Note:** If your group is typically very large and your meeting room is very small, this game could be played outdoors.

Greet students as they arrive and have them form a large circle, facing one another. Bring the chair to the middle of the circle and stand on it so that everyone can see you. Hold your hands out in front of you, one palm up, the other palm down. Demonstrate bringing your hands one over the other (palms together) by moving your arms toward each other. Explain that every time your hands pass one another, students are to clap one time very loudly. There are two ways to be counted out of the game—by not clapping when your hands cross and by clapping when your hands get near each other without crossing.

Ask the adult volunteers to walk around and keep an eye out for the renegade rule breakers. Those caught will be escorted outside the circle to watch the rest of the game. Begin the game and vary the speed so that it's not always easy to tell when your hands are going to cross. The last student remaining in the circle wins. Because it's a fairly quick game, play several rounds for practice, and then play a final round after which you reward the winner(s).

Transition by explaining: **The more you paid attention and obeyed the rules, the longer you got to play. The benefit of obedience in this game was a prize— the benefit of obedience to God in our lives is the opportunity to experience *true* joy, as Jesus knew first-hand.**

STEP 2 MOVING UP

This step teaches students that God loves them and offers them joy when they follow Him.

Option 1 Move It

You'll need Several copies of *the* Book and one copy of this book!

Ask for five volunteers to play the following roles:
- The Vine (God the Son) who will read John 15:1-11
- The Gardener (God the Father)
- Two branches
- The fruit (one or two people) that pop up on the branch that is pruned

Position the vine and have the two branches stand on either side as if connected to the vine. As the vine reads John 15:1-11, the other actors will act according to what's in the passage. The vine should pause as called for to allow actors to play their parts.

After the impromptu drama, award plenty of applause; then discuss:

What happened in this passage? (Get literal details—don't ask students to interpret.)

Who does the Vine represent? Jesus.

Who does the Gardener represent? God.

Who do the branches represent? Believers.

What does the fruit represent? Good character, good works and bringing others to faith in Christ.

What happened to the two branches? One branch was pruned and became more fruitful; one didn't remain on the vine and it was thrown out.

Why did the Gardener do what He did? Because the second one wasn't producing fruit.

How important is it to produce spiritual fruit? Very! It is a sign of the condition of your relationship with the Vine.

According to those verses, what is the source of a Christian's joy? Obeying the commands of God and fulfilling our lives in the way He has called us to do.

Read John 5:19,30 and explain: **Jesus spoke here about His own need to remain in the Father and how He knew that nothing was possible without God. Just as it was essential for Jesus to stay connected to His Father, it's essential that *we* stay connected to Jesus. "Living in Jesus" means more than just believing in Him—it means also remaining in Him by obeying His commands. Just as an orange tree is designed to produce oranges, so are we designed to produce spiritual fruit of godly character, souls won for Christ and good works. When we do, we're joyful because we are fulfilling the life God has called us to live.**

Option 2 — Chat Room

You'll need Several Bibles, a TV, a VCR and the video *The Lion King*.

Ahead of time, cue the video approximately 29 minutes from the opening graphic to the scene where Simba and his friend, Nala, wander into forbidden territory, are chased by hyenas and then rescued by Simba's father, who explains his fear that they might get hurt.

Pair off students and have the pairs discuss a time they disobeyed someone and what happened as a result of their actions. Allow several minutes for discussion; then invite volunteers to share their stories with the whole group.

Set up the video by explaining: **Let's take a look at the importance of obedience to those who love us.**

After the video clip, discuss the following questions.

What happened in this clip? Simba disobeyed his father and went to the forbidden territory. Because of his disobedience, he put himself and his friend in danger. **How can we compare the father in the video to our relationship with our heavenly Father?** They both care deeply about their children and have established rules for them to follow in order to protect them.

Read John 15:1-11 and discuss:

Who is the Vine? Jesus Christ.

Who is the Gardener? God.

What is the Gardener's job? To help the branches be fruitful.

What circumstances are required to make the branch produce fruit? Remaining on the vine.

How is that true in our Christian life? Only by staying connected to Christ will our lives change and will we impact others.

According to these verses, what is the source of a Christian's joy? Obedience to God's will through a relationship with Jesus.

How have you seen that to be true in your own life?

Read John 5:19,30 and explain: **Jesus spoke here about His own need to remain in the Father and how He knew that nothing was possible without God. Just as it was essential for Jesus to stay connected to His Father, it's essential that *we* stay connected to Jesus. "Living in Jesus" means more than just believing in Him—it means also remaining in Him by following His commands. Just as an orange tree is designed to produce oranges, so are we designed to produce fruit through good works. When we do, we're joyful because we are fulfilling the life God has called us to live.**

Option 3  Pulse Points

You'll need Several Bibles, the book *The Hiding Place* by Corrie Ten Boom (a special 25th Anniversary Edition, published in 1996 by Chosen Books, is available at most Christian and secular bookstores), the game Twister, masking or transparent tape, a lunch-size paper bag and a can of soda.

Ahead of time, read *The Hiding Place*—not only to familiarize yourself with it, but also because it's a good book! Place the soda in the paper bag; then fold the top of the bag down so that only the top of the can shows. Tape the bag securely around the can so that no one can see what flavor or brand the soda is.

The Big Idea

Obeying God brings joy to our lives.

The Big Question

What is joy?

1. Joy is different than happiness.

Distribute Bibles and ask a volunteer to read Matthew 5:3-11. Explain: **Those who are blessed are those who know God. They depend on God for joy—not their circumstances.** Give an example of this by reading a section from chapter 13 in *The Hiding Place* where they give thanks for the *fleas* (several pages after the beginning of the chapter look for, "We followed our guide single file . . ." and read for about two pages until, "But this time I was sure Betsie was wrong" and then stop reading). Discuss: **How could Corrie's sister, Betsie, possibly be filled with joy while living in such a horrible environment?** Explain that happiness depends on circumstances, while true joy exists *apart* from the circumstances.

2. Joy is staying connected to God.

Read John 15:1-11 and point out that the vine that bore fruit was fulfilling its purpose. Explain: **When we stay connected to God we fulfill our purpose and receive joy.** Ask for two or three volunteers to play a short game of Twister (three to five minutes, timed). After the time is up, remind students that the goal of the game was to stay connected to the colored pieces. As long as a player did, he or she stayed in the game; if a player didn't, he or she was out. Similarly, the more connected we are to God, the better our lives and the greater our joy.

3. Joy comes from God.

Ask a volunteer to read Romans 15:13; then explain: **This verse shows that God is the one who fills us with joy when we trust in Him.** Offer the soda wrapped in the paper bag to a student who is willing to trust you and drink the soda without knowing what brand or flavor it is. Explain to the group that this student has a choice: either he or she can trust you and enjoy the drink or choose not to trust you and miss out. Explain: **The more we trust God with things we cannot see, the more we will get to drink of His joy.**

STEP 3
MOVING ON

This step helps students recognize that knowing God brings true joy.

Option 1  Chat Room

You'll need One copy of "What's Next?" (p. 38) and a pen or pencil for every three to four students.

Divide students into groups of three or four. Distribute "What's Next?" and a pen or pencil to each group. Instruct students to work in their groups to complete Part One of the handout; then share their responses with the whole group. After a few moments of sharing, read the following story:

> In the early 1800s in Manchester, England, an unhappy and depressed middle-aged man, while traveling, visited a physician who had been recommended to him.
>
> "How may I help you?" the physician asked. The sad-faced man told the physician he was suffering from a hopeless illness. He was in terror of the world around him and nothing gave him pleasure or amused him or gave him a reason to live. "If you can't help me," he told the physician, "I'm afraid I will kill myself."
>
> The physician tried to reassure the man. He told the man that he could be cured. He encouraged him to get out of himself, to find things that would amuse him, cheer him up and make him laugh.
>
> The patient said, "Where can I go to find such a diversion?" The physician replied, "The circus is in town tonight. Go see Grimaldi the clown. Grimaldi is the funniest man alive. He will cure you."
>
> The sad-faced patient looked up and said, "Doctor, I am Grimaldi. I am Grimaldi." [1]

Ask students to work in their groups to complete Part Two of the handout; then conclude by asking each group to share their responses with the entire group.

Option 2  Real Life

You'll need Your Bible and this awesome **Pulse** book!

Read the following testimony from a girl named Jessie:

> I've tried it all. OK, OK, maybe not *everything*, but I've sure tried a lot. I've never been afraid to do things at parties or with friends that I thought might make me feel better about myself. There were lots of times that some of those things worked—but only for a little while. Once I felt good for about a day and a half, but if I wanted to keep feeling that way, I would have to do it again. I figured that would get old. My friends thought I was cool, but I didn't think that it was worth the hassle.
>
> So now, I guess I'm looking for some help again. I've been coming to this church for a while and even though I'm not sure about all of this Jesus stuff, I am interested. I guess I'm just afraid that it won't last. I mean maybe it'll last longer than a day and a half—but what good is it if it lasts even a year and then I'm stuck with nothing—again? So that's me. I'm looking for answers and hoping to find some. I want to believe in this whole Jesus deal—but is it for me?

Discuss:
What advice would you give to Jessie?
What do you think God might have to say to her?
Does being a Christian mean that you'll never feel bad again? No way! Christian or not, we are all human beings with emotions and problems. The difference is that being a Christian means we can look up and ask God for help when we're feeling bad, and we know that He is right there with us to see us through the hard times.
Have you ever felt like Jessie?
How did you deal with those feelings?
Knowing what you know now, what would you like to do differently in the future?

Option 3  Tough Questions

You'll need These questions and some students to discuss them with!

1. **How can I be joyful when I'm having a rotten day or month and I feel unhappy?** Happiness is something that emerges from what's *happen*ing to us. That means if we're having a good day, we'll be happy; if not, we won't. In contrast, *joy* is based on something more solid—our relationship with God and our ability to thank Him even when what's happening to us isn't fun. First Thessalonians 5:18 says that we should "give thanks in all circumstances, for this is God's will for you in Christ Jesus." That means we can choose to be joyful and thankful for small things even when we're in the middle of a bad day.

2. **What if I don't feel like being joyful?** Being joyful is a choice. You may not feel good about being in a tough situation, but when you choose to be joyful, you are making a choice in how you respond to it. Joy is a process; it's not a magic pill.

3. **How can I help people I care about to be joyful?** We can't force others to be joyful because it is a choice. Since it's God who brings joy, people have to be willing to open up to His gift. We can help people in our lives to experience the joy God offers by praying for them and by setting an example of being joyful during tough times in our own lives.

5. **Is knowing God the only way to be joyful?** Knowing God is the only way to *true* joy. Other things or people can bring temporary happiness to our lives, but God is the only one who can bring true joy.

6. **What's one thing I can do to live a joyful life?** Actually, we can find joy in serving others! When we get our minds off of our own problems and focus on loving God by loving people, God will give us joy.

STEP 4  MOVING OUT

This step invites students to experience real joy by dedicating (or rededicating) their lives to Christ.

Option 1  Light the Fire

You'll need Several gift Bibles, lots of first-aid supplies (a variety of bandages, creams, hydrogen peroxide, etc.) and a table.

Ahead of time, arrange the supplies on the table.

Call attention to the first-aid supplies on the table and explain the purpose of each item and show how it might be used to help an injured person. Explain that before a person's wound is covered, it must first be cleaned out and then covered with antiseptic and a bandage. Otherwise, it will not heal.

Explain: **We all have spiritual wounds from sin—our own sins, and the sins others have committed against us. These wounds will keep us from having a healthy relationship with our heavenly Father, and no physical ointment or bandage in the world can possibly heal them. There is only one way for our sin wounds to heal and for us to follow God's plan for a relationship with Him. That way is through the wounds Christ suffered on the cross for each of us—because "by his wounds we are healed" (Isaiah 53:5, see also 1 Peter 2:24).**

No matter what happens in your life, if you will continue to turn your wounds over to Jesus Christ, you will have healing forever. This doesn't mean that your life will be totally perfect, but it does mean that in the imperfection of life, you will have total perfect joy in Christ. All you have to do to receive His healing is to repent from your sins and invite Him into your life to transform and heal you. Then start making lots of choices for Jesus, determining to follow Him in the little and big things in your life.

Invite students who would like to commit (or recommit) their lives to Jesus to repeat the following prayer to themselves as you pray aloud: **Dear Jesus, I know that my sin separates me from You. I know that I need to** be healed from the spiritual wounds caused by my sin and that You are the cure for those wounds. I invite You to come into my heart and take over my life and heal the pain of these wounds. Thank You for loving me enough to die on the Cross for my sins and help me to follow Your will for my life. Amen.

Invite anyone who prayed that prayer for the first time (or who renewed their commitment) to come forward. Give each of them a gift Bible and write down their names and phone numbers. Be sure to follow up by contacting each of them this week and encouraging them to continue in their new walk with Christ.

Option 2 Fired Up

You'll need Copies of "If the Shoe Fits" (p. 39) and pens or pencils. **Option:** Shoes as described in the handout to use as a visual aid.

Distribute "If the Shoe Fits" and pens or pencils. If you brought shoes for a visual aid, point out the description of each on the handout. If you opted not to bring shoes, that's OK! Either way, instruct students to complete their handouts and allow time to do so. After a few minutes, invite willing students to share what they wrote.

Close in prayer, thanking God that regardless of the state we're in, He loves us and wants to have a relationship with us that will bring us joy in our lives.

Option 3 Spread the Fire

You'll need A white board, a dry-erase marker, paper, pens or pencils and a list of service opportunities.

Ahead of time, research any service opportunities in your area and compile a reference list. [2]

Explain: **One way to demonstrate that we've given our lives to Christ and show the joy He's given us is by serving others.**

Divide students into groups of five or six and distribute a piece of paper and a pen or pencil to each group. Ask groups to brainstorm as many possible service opportunities as they can in their community and in surrounding communities.

Allow three to five minutes for brainstorming; then invite groups to share their ideas. Write each different idea on the white board and then call for a show of hands to vote for the top five ideas.

Compare the top five ideas to the list you compiled earlier and share the ones you researched; then add the top five ideas to your list for future reference. Call for another vote on which project students would like to do and decide on a date to do it! Take names of students willing to help coordinate the details and be sure to meet regularly to get the project scheduled and underway.

Close in prayer, thanking God for the opportunity to share His love with others through service and asking Him to bless students with ample opportunities to serve others.

Notes
1. Adapted from Jim Burns and Greg McKinnon, *Fresh Ideas: Illustrations, Stories, and Quotes* (Ventura, CA: Gospel Light, 1997), p. 59.
2. **Suggestion:** *Fresh Ideas: Missions and Service Projects* by Jim Burns and Mike DeVries (Ventura, CA: Gospel Light, 1999) is a great resource for projects.

NOTES

Following Directions

Read through the entire test before answering questions. Answer each question in sequence. If you do not know an answer, skip it and proceed to the next one.

1. Print your complete name in the upper left-hand corner.

2. Print your address in the space below:

3. Circle the correct answer to complete each statement:
    - A smart person must (study, interview other smart people, watch a lot of TV).
    - The greatest sign of intelligence is (high grades, respect for others, use of big words).
    - The best way to become intelligent is to read (magazines, cereal boxes, the encyclopedia).

4. Print your age in the upper right-hand corner.

5. Raise your right hand until you are recognized by the leader.

6. Circle the correct answer:
    - A smart person always has an answer.   True or False
    - A smart person knows how to follow directions.   True or False
    - A smart person gets things done quickly.   True or False
    - It is better to do a job right than quickly.   True or False

7. Underline the words "follow directions" in question six.

8. Stand up until you are recognized by your leader.

9. In the left margin of this page, write the first and last names of five people who you consider to be intelligent.

10. You do not have to do any of the above activities, except number one.

What's Next?

Part One

Is there a difference between joy and happiness? What is it?

Is it possible to have a bad day but still be filled with joy?

What would you say to someone who wants to find joy in his or her life?

Part Two

What is the point of the story about Grimaldi?

Read the following verses and on the back of this handout, write what it says gives true joy in life:

"The thief comes only to steal and kill and destroy; I have come that they may have life, and have it to the full" (John 10:10).

"As the Father has loved me, so have I loved you. Now remain in my love. If you obey my commands, you will remain in my love, just as I have obeyed my Father's commands and remain in his love. I have told you this so that my joy may be in you and that your joy may be complete" (John 15:9-11).

If Grimaldi had asked for your advice, what would you have said?

How do you feel about the joy that comes from your own relationship with God?

If the Shoe Fits*

Put a ✔ (check mark) next to the shoe that best describes your current spiritual condition. Circle the shoe that you'd like to describe your spiritual life.

☐ **Dress shoes:** I have a nice, shiny faith on the outside—but I only bring it out on Sundays and special occasions.

☐ **Basketball shoes:** I feel like God is helping me compete and win.

☐ **Slippers:** I've made a commitment to Christ, but I've been pretty lazy in terms of trying to serve Him.

☐ **Tired shoes:** I've come a long way, but I'm well worn and need some serious "heeling."

☐ **Work boots:** It's been hard work lately, but I'm actually following through on my responsibilities.

☐ **Swiss-cheese (holey) shoes:** I don't worry too much about a relationship with God or the state of my sole (soul).

What steps can you take to reach the pair of shoes you checked?

Who can you ask to walk with you?

* Adapted from *Everyday Object Lessons for Youth Groups*, Helen Musick and Duffy Robbins. Copyright ©1999 by Youth Specialties, Inc. Used by permission of Zondervan Publishing House.

Devotions in Motion

WEEK TWO: JOY

DAY 1

QUICK QUESTIONS

Make a beeline for Psalm 16:11.

God Says

Imagine you come home from school, grab a snack, then flop on your bed. You're just lying there relaxing when you notice your Bible on the floor and remember what you heard in church about receiving joy as you spend time with God. What do you do?

- ☐ Decide to play video games because they're so much fun.
- ☐ Convince yourself you'll read it later—maybe.
- ☐ Pick it up and flip through it casually just to see if something catches your eye.
- ☐ Pick it up excitedly because you can't wait to spend time with God.

I Do

How do you feel about spending time with God?

Do you look forward to it or does it feel like a chore?

What can you do to want to know and obey God more?

Do you know Christians who seem to be continually joyful? Ask them to teach you how they spend time with God.

FOLD HERE ---

DAY 4

FAST FACTS

Sing a song as you read Philippians 4:4.

God Says

Beth had saved her baby-sitting money for quite a while and when she had enough to buy some new outfits, her mom took her shopping.

"It's my money! I should be able to buy what I want!" Beth shouted as she stormed into the house when they returned. She desperately wanted to wear dresses like the popular girls at school, but her mom refused to let her buy the one she found because it was too revealing. Beth was beside herself with frustration and ran to her room, slamming the door.

After some cooling-off time, Beth came out of her room and went looking for her mom. When she found her, Beth apologized for her behavior and said, "I know you only want me to look my best, Mom. I want to fit in at school and with my friends, but I'm OK with not having that dress. Do you think we could try shopping again sometime and see if we can find something that we both like?" Her mom just smiled and gave her a big, understanding hug.

I Do

Because of Jesus, you can have joy all the time—even when things don't seem to be going your way. Knowing Jesus is way better than owning the right outfit, and this joy outweighs fitting in with the right group at school.

Is there an area of your life over which it's hard to rejoice?

Ask Jesus to help you rejoice in Him.

FAST FACTS

Read Proverbs 10:28. It's a gold mine!

God Says

Taylor had worked really hard on his science project even though the rest of his group hadn't. Today in science class, Mrs. Henderson returned the projects and passed out the grades. Taylor hoped that she would be able to tell how much effort he'd put into it and not lower his grade because the others hadn't helped.

Taylor held his breath as Mrs. Henderson handed him his paper. An A—whew! After class, his partners pulled Taylor aside because they hadn't done well and learning about Taylor's A really made them angry. "We should all have gotten the same grade!" they ranted. "It's our project, not just yours!" Taylor muttered to himself, "That might be true, but I did most of the work."

I Do

God wants you to do the right thing, and He promises joy as a result. Even though you might not always get the outcome you'd hoped for—Mrs. Henderson could have given each of the partners the same grade, which might have made the other partners happy, but would have been less fair to Taylor—but you'll still have the joy of knowing that you did what God wanted you to do. In Taylor's case, he honored God by doing his best on the project even when no one else was interested in helping.

Look in your Bible for something God wants you to do; then figure out how you can do it this week.

QUICK QUESTIONS

Read about the joyful jailer in Acts 16:34.

God Says

There's a knock at your door. You open it to find some very enthusiastic people who want to tell you about the secret of Time Travel! Skeptical but interested, you sit on the porch and listen as they share rich stories of their travels. Then they tell you the best part—all you have to do is believe and this amazing power of Time Travel is all yours! What is your reaction?

☐ You feel like your heart will burst as you consider the wonders of your new ability.

☐ You laugh as you go inside and shut the door.

☐ You ponder their tales but don't commit to believing anything.

It would be totally cool to really be able to Time Travel, wouldn't it? Would you believe that there is something even better? Knowing the One who actually created Time itself?! What's the key? Just believe in Him and accept Him as your Lord and Savior, Jesus Christ.

I Do

Do you remember when you first believed in God? How did it make you feel? Do you feel any different about God now? Why or why not?

Would you like to feel more joy in your relationship with God? The jailer served Paul and Silas a meal to say thank you for telling him about God. Try serving someone and see if you experience joy as a result.

FOLD HERE

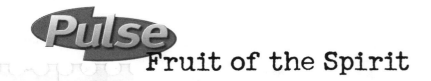

Fruit of the Spirit

The Big Idea

Peace through Jesus Christ is a true peace that is always available.

Session Aims

In this session you will guide students to:

- Understand that Jesus is always with them;
- Realize that Jesus always offers them peace;
- Receive the peace Jesus offers by bringing everything to Him in prayer.

The Biggest Verse

"On the evening of that first day of the week, when the disciples were together, with the doors locked for fear of the Jews, Jesus came and stood among them and said, 'Peace be with you!'" John 20:19

Other Important Verses

2 Chronicles 14:7; Psalm 4:8; 29:11; Matthew 5:23-26; John 14:14-18,27; 16:31-33; 20:19-23; Philippians 4:6,7; 1 Peter 3:11; 1 John 1:8-10

Peace

STEP MOVING IN

This step reminds students that without Christ, true peace is impossible to experience.

Option 1  Move It

You'll need Large peel-and-stick labels (available at any office supply store) and pens or pencils.

Welcome students and discuss: **What are some different ways that people seek peace in their lives?**

Distribute labels and pens or pencils and ask students to write down one way (e.g., partying, listen to music, praying, going camping, etc.) that someone might seek peace. *Without showing or telling what they wrote*, have students stick their labels on each other's backs.

Explain that when you give the signal, students are to go around the room and ask only yes-or-no questions to find out what the labels on their backs say. Once everyone has figured out his or her label (or after a few minutes), discuss the different ways people try to get peace in their lives and discuss which ones, if any, students believe are effective.

Transition to the next step by explaining: **There are a number of ways people seek peace in their lives, and today we're going to look at what the Bible says about the best way to find peace.**

Option 2  Chat Room

You'll need A guest to speak to your students. Choose someone who has been through some pretty tough circumstances in life, yet lives a joy-filled life of peace.

Ahead of time, arrange for the guest to wait outside the room until you are ready for him or her to come in.

Greet students and let them know that you've invited a guest to share insights about his or her life and how it relates to the topic of peace. Offer an overview of who the guest is and why you have asked him or her to speak; then divide students into groups of four or five and have them brainstorm questions to ask the guest. Each group should come up with at least five questions.

Invite the guest to come into the room and share his or her story and what his or her life is like as a Christian. Allow students to ask the questions that the small groups came up with.

Transition by explaining: **Having peace in our lives is only possible if we have a growing relationship with Jesus Christ. The world offers many ways to obtain peace outside of Christ, but they all fall short. Let's take a look at what the Bible says on this topic.**

Option 3  Fun and Games

You'll need Paper, pens or pencils and a die for each group of five to eight students.

Ahead of time, practice playing Manners, so you're familiar with it. (This is actually an easy game to play; playing it beforehand will help you to be able to explain it.)

Welcome students and divide them into teams of five to eight. Distribute one die, paper and a pen or pencil to each group. Explain that students are going to play Manners, a game where the object is to be the first team to write the numbers 1 to 100 on its paper. Since each team only has one pen or pencil, only one person can write at a time.

Here are the rules: The teams begin the game by having one person roll the die; then passing it to the next person. When a teammate rolls a one or a six, he or she gets to begin writing the numerals from 1 to 100 on the paper (they must write the actual numbers). He or she continues numbering until someone else rolls a one or a six; then that group member takes over the numbering, continuing where the last player left off (if the previous player stopped at 16, the current player begins with 17, etc.). Once a player reaches 80, he or she must say each number aloud as it's written, allowing everyone in the group to know where he's at (which creates plenty of tension between the teams!).

Begin the game. Once a team reaches 100, stop the game and point out the irony of the game's name—Manners—since it's played in a way where few manners are used!

Transition by explaining: **Expecting to find manners in this game is similar to looking for peace through** worldly things such as things we own, people we know or things we do. Let's take a look at how to find true peace by checking out what the Bible has to say on the topic.

STEP 2 — MOVING UP

This step teaches students that Christ is the only One who offers true peace.

Option 1 — Move It

You'll need Several Bibles and a bunch of newspapers and magazines.

Distribute newspapers and magazines and invite students to look through them and find as many things as they can that represent problems in the world (war, arguments, protests, etc.), including advertisements, movie titles and articles.

Allow several minutes for discovering items; then discuss what students found, the cause of each conflict and how it might be resolved. After discussing items found, invite students to discuss conflicts that are happening in their schools or local communities and possible resolutions for those, too.

Distribute Bibles and ask a volunteer to read John 20:19-23. Discuss:

What significant event had just happened? Jesus had been crucified in public.

How might Jesus' friends have felt at the time? Abandoned, alone, scared.

Why did Jesus say "Peace be with you" two separate times? This was a common greeting during biblical times, but when Jesus spoke it, He was speaking of the true peace that would come now that His work on the cross was finished.

How did Jesus offer peace to His friends? He showed them that He had been resurrected and that He would be with them forever.

What does the presence of Jesus do for His friends? It comforts them and puts them into position to spread the truth about Jesus.

Has there been a time in your life when you felt comforted by the presence of Jesus? Allow a few students to describe times of peace.

Explain: **The fact that in His resurrection body Jesus got past locked doors shows that He was no longer bound by the same laws of nature that we are. After the resurrection, Jesus ascended to heaven at the right hand of the Father—but He did not leave us alone. He kept His promise that we would not be like orphans and sent the Holy Spirit to be with us** (see John 14:14-18). **The peace of Jesus Christ can be with us in the midst of complete turmoil in our lives.**

NOTES

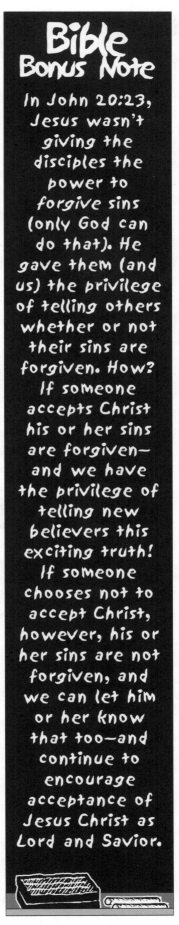

Bible Bonus Note

In John 20:23, Jesus wasn't giving the disciples the power to forgive sins (only God can do that). He gave them (and us) the privilege of telling others whether or not their sins are forgiven. How? If someone accepts Christ his or her sins are forgiven—and we have the privilege of telling new believers this exciting truth! If someone chooses not to accept Christ, however, his or her sins are not forgiven, and we can let him or her know that too—and continue to encourage acceptance of Jesus Christ as Lord and Savior.

Option 2  Chat Room

You'll need Several Bibles, six 3x5-inch index cards for every four to six students, a box or other container and pens or pencils.

Divide students into groups of four to six and distribute Bibles, index cards and pens or pencils; then instruct groups to read John 20:19-23 and summarize the passage on one of their index cards. On each of the remaining cards, they are to write a question about the passage on one side and the answer to that question on the other side. Have students put their names on their question cards.

Allow a few minutes for groups to complete their cards; then collect all of the question cards and place them in the box (each group needs to keep its summary card). One at a time, have each group read its summary card and as they are read, discuss each summary, being sure to clarify any misunderstandings the groups may have had about the passage.

After all the summary cards have been discussed, use the question cards to have a contest to see which group can answer the most questions correctly. Give 10 points to the quickest *correct* response. The groups cannot answer their own questions (that's why they signed their question cards. Pull one card out of the box and begin the contest by reading the question aloud. Continue until all the questions have been answered and tally up the points to determine the winning team. Discuss:

What significant event had just happened in this passage? Jesus had been crucified in public.

How might Jesus' friends have felt at the time? Abandoned, alone, scared.

Why did Jesus say "Peace be with you" two separate times? This was a common greeting during biblical times, but when Jesus spoke it, He was speaking of the true peace that would come now that His work on the cross was finished.

How did Jesus offer peace to His friends? He showed them that He had been resurrected.

What does the presence of Jesus do for His friends? It comforts them and positions them to be sent by Jesus to spread the truth about Him.

Describe a time when you felt comforted by the presence of Jesus.

Explain: **Among other things, the fact that Jesus got past locked doors shows that He is not bound by the** same laws of nature that we are—He can go anywhere at anytime. His peace can be with us in the midst of complete turmoil in our lives.

Option 3  Pulse Points

You'll need Your Bible, a pillow, a football helmet, movie ads from a newspaper and pictures of a foal and a full-grown horse.

The Big Idea
Jesus is the one who offers true peace.

The Big Question
What is peace and why would I want it?

1. Peace gives us rest.
Read Psalm 4:8 and talk about the rest we get when we lie down to sleep and have peace with God. Compare that to trying to sleep after watching a horror movie. Show ads in the newspaper of current scary movies, and ask students what is the scariest movie they've ever seen. Discuss whether or not that movie affected their sleep; then read Psalm 4:8 again and emphasize the peace God provides.

2. Peace gives us strength.
Hold up the pictures of the foal and the horse and discuss the strength that a full-grown horse has compared to a helpless foal; how a foal can barely hold its own weight and is really wobbly. Yet that same foal, when full grown, is able to carry hundreds of pounds—and will weigh 900 to 1,200 pounds itself! Read Psalm 29:11 and explain: **Just as the horse grows in strength as it matures, we also grow in strength and peace as we mature in our faith and trust in God.**

3. Peace gives us comfort.
Read John 14:27 and John 16:31-33. Hold up the pillow and illustrate: **This pillow is simply cloth on the outside. It's what's inside the cloth (the stuffing) that makes it special and gives us comfort when we sleep. The same is true with Christians. We're ordinary human beings, but because we have Christ in us, we've got something special that will give our hearts comfort and rest.**

4. Peace gives us confidence.
Ask a volunteer to put on the football helmet. Read

Philippians 4:6,7; then rap on the helmet a couple of times to illustrate the protection it gives. Explain: **The peace God gives us when we pray is like a football helmet. When we pray we can be confident that God will provide peace and offer protection from worry and fear.**

STEP 3
MOVING ON

This step helps students know that of all the options offering temporary peace, none satisfies like Christ's peace.

Option 1  Chat Room

You'll need Several Bibles and someone unfamiliar to students to share a made-up testimony and his real testimony.

Ahead of time, brainstorm a testimony that involves less-than-good behavior such as drugs, alcohol, etc. and be sure to go over any illustrations that will be given so that you aren't caught off guard with anything inappropriate for the students.

Introduce the guest speaker and explain that he is going to share how he found peace with God after being involved with drugs, alcohol, etc. The speaker should start sharing his testimony; then stop and confess that he still regularly uses alcohol and occasionally uses drugs. He should explain that he knows he shouldn't do those things and that he feels really guilty about doing them, but he is afraid to truly trust that God can give peace greater than the temporary, immediate peace that doing those things brings.

Distribute Bibles and divide students into groups of four to six. Instruct students to review Psalms 4:8; 29:11; John 14:27; 16:31-33; and Philippians 4:6,7 and come up with at least three reasons why the guest speaker should fully rely on God for true peace in his life.

After several minutes, ask groups to share their findings and allow the speaker to challenge their thinking. When the discussions are finished, explain that the testimony the guest speaker shared was made up and designed to

get students thinking about alternatives to seeking peace through God; then ask the speaker to share his *true* testimony. Make sure to affirm students for their critical thinking during the exercise.

Option 2  Real Life

You'll need A TV and VCR and a copy of *Hope Floats.*

Ahead of time, cue the video approximately one hour and 43 minutes from the opening graphic to the scene in which Birdee and her husband argue while their daughter clings to her father in fear that she will never see him again. As he drives away, Birdee picks up their daughter and attempts to comfort her.

> **Note:** This video is rated PG-13, which means you should pay extra attention to any objectionable language or content as you show this carefully selected scene to students.

> CAUTION
> While this is a good video clip, it's also a powerful one. Be sure to preview it so that you know the content. Many students will be affected because of the nature of the content (parents splitting up, child caught in the middle). Prepare ahead of time and lead the discussion accordingly.

Share that the options for seeking peace continue all the way through our lives. Explain: **We're going to take a look at a video clip right now that shows a marriage breaking up and a little girl caught in the middle.** Show the clip; then discuss:

How are the mom and dad attempting to find peace in their lives? Avoid dealing with their relationship problems by getting divorced and starting a new life.

What message are they sending to their daughter regarding dealing with conflict? Avoid problems and hope they go away.

What message are they sending about finding peace in life? Peace is available without God's help.

What might you say to the little girl? Learn from your parents' mistakes; choose to follow God's plan.

What might you say to the mom and dad? You will never find what you're looking for outside of doing things God's way.

How would Christ's peace make a difference in this situation? The peace of God makes us whole. When we are whole we can truly enjoy life and relationships with others.

Option 3 — Tough Questions

You'll need Your Bible.

1. **What now? I tried to find peace outside of God and now I feel crummy.** First of all, remember that God always loves you, even when you blow it. Talk with Him and get things right with Him (see 1 John 1:8-10) and with anyone else involved.

2. **Is peace supposed to be a time of rest?** Sometimes. Other times, peace comes through following through on a big commitment that involves lots of hard work. Read 2 Chronicles 14:7 for a picture of how God provided peace by having someone work hard!

3. **Which is more important: making peace with God or making peace with others?** Both are essential! In fact, in Matthew 5:23-26 Jesus instructs us to make things right with others before we spend time worshiping God. God is very concerned that we are at peace in our relationships—with Him and with others.

4. **How do I get peace? Do I just ask for it?** First Peter 3:11 tells us that we are to pursue it—it's a choice. That means intentionally spending time with people who bring peace and rest into our lives, and you know who does that best. God, of course!

NOTES

STEP 4 — MOVING OUT

This step reminds students that they have to seek peace if they want it.

Option 1 — Light the Fire

You'll need Several Bibles, copies of "Give Peace a Chance!" (p. 50) and pens or pencils.

Distribute Bibles, "Give Peace a Chance!" and pens or pencils as you explain that you have a tough assignment for students to accomplish during the next week. Ask if anyone is up to the challenge of watching TV, reading magazines or going to the movies (tough one, huh?). You shouldn't have *too* many protestors.

Ask for a volunteer to read John 14:27; then divide students into groups of four to six and instruct them to complete *only* Part One of the handout in their small groups. Allow three minutes; then ask for volunteers to share their lists. Explain that the remainder of the handout is to be filled out throughout the week as students identify different ways that people seek peace in their lives outside of a relationship with Jesus Christ.

Close in prayer, thanking God for the true peace that only comes through knowing Him and asking Him to continue to show His peace in the midst of earthly problems and temptations.

Option 2 — Fired Up

You'll need A Polaroid camera, enough film to take a picture of every student, a box, 3x5-inch index cards, transparent tape and pens or pencils.

Distribute index cards and pens or pencils and instruct students to write their names and phone numbers on their cards and draw a vertical line down the middle of the card. On the left side of the line, have them write down as many ways they can think of that they're tempted to pursue peace outside of God. On the right side, have them write down ways that help them overcome temptation. (Be ready with some examples of your own in case students get stuck.)

While students are filling out their cards, walk around and take a picture of each student with the camera. When the pictures are dry, have students tape their index cards to the back of their pictures. Finally, collect all of the pictures, place them in the box and one at a time, have students reach in without looking and pick a picture from the box. If they get their own picture, have them try again.

Challenge students to pray for the person whose picture they've chosen (praying for the person's written requests on the back) and invite them to call the person they're praying for during the week to encourage him or her.

Option 3  Spread the Fire

You'll need A box, 3x5-inch index cards and pens or pencils.

Ask students to suggest some possible ways to apply today's lesson (i.e., not being so anxious, praying with people who lack peace, trusting God when your life seems out of control or chaotic). Encourage different levels of application, from easy to difficult. After several examples have been shared, give each student four or five index cards and a pen or pencil. Tell them you're going to play "I Dare You!" Have them write down one possible way to apply the lesson on each card. As you did earlier, encourage them to have a range of applications, but choose ideas that could actually be accomplished this week.

Have all of the students place their cards in the box and give them the following directions: **Reach into the box, choose one card and read it out loud. At that time, you can choose to accept that challenge or choose another card. If you don't want to accept the challenge from the second card, you may choose a third card, but then you must keep one of the three cards or trade with someone else. When you have chosen an action, share out loud how obeying that action might give you an opportunity to share your faith or be an example or witness for someone who doesn't know Jesus yet.**

Conclude by having students pray in small groups for strength to follow through on their chosen action.

NOTES

Give Peace a Chance!

PART ONE

List five ways that TV or movies show how people get peace in their lives; then place a ✔ next to the things you've been tempted to participate in.

❑ _____

❑ _____

❑ _____

❑ _____

❑ _____

How have you avoided these temptations (or others) in the past?

What area of temptation do you need prayer for this week?

PART TWO

As you notice ways that movies, TV shows and magazines encourage people to find peace in their lives, write them below. Next to each example, write down why that example won't bring true, lasting peace.

1. _____

2. _____

3. _____

4. _____

5. _____

6. _____

7. _____

8. _____

9. _____

10. _____

Devotions in Motion

WEEK THREE: PEACE

DAY 1

QUICK QUESTIONS

Sleep Tight, but read Psalm 4:8 first.

God Says

Raised totally in the city, you're invited to go on a camping trip with your friend and his family. This is all new to you; you've never even slept outside before! Your friend shows you how to set up the tent. The two of you are sharing and you get to help catch the fresh fish and cook it over the campfire. You especially enjoy telling stories and making s'mores around the campfire. This evening under the stars.

You're lying in your sleeping bag exhausted but wide awake. Your friend is already snoring. What do you do now?

☐ Lie there, anxiously listening to all the new sounds—the owl, the crickets, the breeze and the bear you're sure you hear sniffing around the tent.

☐ Drift off into a deep slumber, anticipating tomorrow's adventures.

☐ Try counting sheep; then give up and wake up your friend to keep you company.

I Do

What keeps you awake at night?

How do those things relate to anxiety?

What do you do when you can't sleep?

Memorize Psalm 4:8 and pray it each night before you go to sleep.

DAY 4

FAST FACTS

Quick, like a Tiger! Read 2 Timothy 2:22.

God Says

Ben felt like Dr. Jekyll and Mr. Hyde. At school, he found himself saying mean things to people, gossiping, laughing at dirty jokes, shoving people out of his way—generally being a total jerk. He didn't like the way he acted, but he couldn't seem to stop.

But, when he was with his friends from church, Ben didn't do any of the rotten things he did in school. Instead, he tried to encourage his friends. He never said anything that needed to be followed up with "just kidding." He liked himself better when he spent time with other Christians, and his friendships with them felt better than the relationships he had with kids at school.

I Do

Friends have a huge influence over us, whether we like to admit it or not. It's just easier to follow Christ and pursue peace when you spend time with others who do the same.

This week make an effort to fellowship with other Christians—or even invite one of your non-Christian friends to come to church with you—you might find you're a more peaceful person for it.

FAST FACTS

Get closer to Jesus as you read Ephesians 2:17.

God Says

With her friends, Tracy felt so peaceful. She never told lies or passed on rumors or fought with them—and when her friends fought with each other, they relied on Tracy to help them make up.

With her brother and sister, however, it was a very different story. Tracy borrowed her sister's clothes and her brother's CDs without asking. When their parents wanted to know who'd left dishes in front of the TV, Tracy lied and blamed it on her siblings. She listened in on their phone conversations and then got mad when they did the same thing to her. Hardly a family meal went by without an argument over something.

I Do

Why does it seem hardest to be peaceful with those we are closest to?

Jesus wants you to be at peace with everyone, including your family. Next time you're tempted to talk back to a family member, imagine Jesus has His hand in front of your mouth; then smile instead!

FOLD HERE

QUICK QUESTIONS

Learn how not to stress in Philippians 4:6,7.

God Says

You're in your room one afternoon slaving over your homework when your mom knocks at your door. "We need to talk," she says.

As you listen, you learn that your mom has just returned from seeing a doctor and that, even though she needs more tests to confirm it, her doctor thinks she might have cancer.

No one is sure how serious your mom's illness might be; they're pretty sure it's not life threatening, but it definitely could mean changes for your family. You'll at least have to help out more around the house while your mom tries to rest; and you won't have any extra spending money while your parents try to manage extra medical bills.

I Do

What worries you most (school, parents, friends, the future, etc.)?

How can prayer help you not to be anxious about those things?

Why do you think God gives peace in return for prayer? How can you remind yourself to pray, rather than get anxious?

Why do you think God guards both your heart and your mind?

Try keeping a prayer journal. Write down what you're worried about in the form of a prayer; then keep track of what God does about your worries.

The Big Idea

Jesus gives us the ultimate example of faithfulness when He remains ever faithful, even when we aren't.

Session Aims

In this session you will guide students to:

- Understand that God will never leave them or forsake them;
- Feel secure in their relationship with God;
- Act like a faithful friend and family member this week.

The Biggest Verse

"God, who has called you into fellowship with his Son Jesus Christ our Lord, is faithful."
1 Corinthians 1:9

Faithfulness

Other Important Verses

Deuteronomy 31:6; Job 1:21,22;
Proverbs 3:3-6; 17:17; 18:24;
Lamentations 3:22,23; Zechariah 13:7;
Matthew 28:20; Mark 14:27-31,66-72;
John 3:16; 10:28,29; 15:13;
Romans 5:8; 7:7-26; 8:1,38,39;
1 Corinthians 1:9; 10:13;
1 Thessalonians 5:24; Hebrews 7:25;
1 John 1:9; 3:2,16; 4:8,16

STEP

MOVING IN

This step reminds students that it's a powerful feeling to belong.

Option 1  Move It

You'll need A current list of the top-selling secular and Christian songs, 3x5-inch index cards (or slips of paper), pens or pencils and either an audiotape recorder and audiotape *or* a VCR, a blank videocassette and a TV.

Ahead of time, create an audiotape or videotape of a music "Top 10" (or 20, 30, 40) show that plays each of the songs (choose secular or Christian songs, depending on the makeup of your group—or a combination of the two). After you've done that, edit bits and pieces of each song on another tape that you will play to the students.

Also ahead of time, list the artists and titles of songs you record for your own reference during the activity.

Welcome students and divide them into four groups; then separate the groups so that each has some privacy during the exercise (but where they can all hear the tape or see the video). As you distribute index cards and pens or pencils, explain that you are going to play a tape (or video) that has recent top-of-the-chart songs on it. Groups will identify the song and artist of as many of the songs as they can and one person in each group will write down his or her group's answers.

After you've played the tape, call out the correct answers and have groups tally up their correct answers. The group with the most correct answers wins.

Announce the winners; then instruct groups to read through their lists and come up with the theme, or main point, of each song. Allow a few minutes for groups to work; then ask the whole group which themes are repeated most frequently. Most of the songs will deal with some sort of a relationship (with a person or with God) or an intense emotion (love, hate, fear, jealousy, etc.).

Discuss: **Why does it seem that relationships make up the theme of so many songs?** Ask what they feel is the condition of most of those relationships the singers are singing about, and have students suggest how they might make those relationships healthier.

Transition to the next step by saying: **Today we're going to study relationships and how powerful it feels to be in a healthy one. We're also going to focus on a key characteristic that all healthy relationships have: faithfulness. As we'll see, the Bible has a lot to say about how we can be faithful to God and each other.**

NOTES

Option 2  Chat Room

You'll need A **Pulse**—this one to be exact!

Greet students and divide them into groups of four or five. Explain that you're going to have them respond in different ways to some questions about their life experiences; then, depending on their responses, they're going to discuss the scenarios in their small groups. Use the following scenarios and make sure to pause between scenarios for small group discussion:

If you know someone who has a close friend, stand up. Have students discuss how they think that person feels to have such a close friend.

If you know someone with a close-knit family, say "hello" to the person next to you. Have students discuss ways that families show they are close.

If you know someone who has a difficult family situation, shout the name of your favorite dessert. Have students discuss how that person must feel.

If you've ever felt connected to a certain group, share the name of your least favorite food. Have students share what it's like to be connected to a group and how that made them feel.

If you've ever felt like you didn't belong somewhere, whisper to the person next to you the name of your favorite place to go. Have students discuss what it was like and what they learned from it.

Transition to the next step by explaining: **Belonging to a group or being in a relationship is important for all of us. Today we're going to look at how being a faithful friend can help others feel like they belong and how we can know that God is always faithful in His relationship with us.**

Option 3  Fun and Games

You'll need Two buckets and several round balloons.

Ahead of time, blow up two of the balloons (keep the others ready as standbys).

Welcome students and divide them into two teams on opposite ends of the room. Have teammates line up side by side; then select three people from each team as the players to begin the game. Give one of the three from each team a bucket and instruct him or her to stand at the end of the room opposite his or her team; then give a balloon to another of the three.

Explain: **When you say "Go," the two from each team without the bucket will volley a balloon back and forth until they can get it into the bucket. Here's the catch: they cannot carry the balloon and neither can hit it two times in a row. The bucket holder may move the bucket to make it easier to catch the balloon, but must continue to stand in the same spot at all times.**

Every time the balloon is successfully caught in the bucket, the volleying players will race the balloon back to the starting line and the next person in line joins the volleying. The three of them will now work to get the balloon into the bucket. With more people helping, it should increase the speed of the scoring, but life is sometimes full of surprises. Choose a designated amount of time for playing each round—one to two minutes works well. The goal is to have the most people in the game when the time is up and you give the signal to stop.

After a few rounds, ask for a show of hands by people who didn't get to play or just briefly played. Discuss:

Did anyone who played the game quite a bit notice that there were others who weren't playing as much? How do you think those students might have felt on the sidelines? Left out, ignored, unimportant.

Ask students who didn't get to play or played only briefly:

How did it feel to watch instead of play? Did you enjoy the game anyway? Probably not as much as they would have if they had played more.

Transition to the next step by explaining: **Just as it's usually more fun to play a game than it is to watch, having a close friend or belonging to a group makes us feel good about ourselves. Today we're going to look at what it means to be a faithful person, and what that looks like in our relationships with one another and God. As we'll see, the Bible has a lot to say about how we can be faithful to God and others.**

NOTES

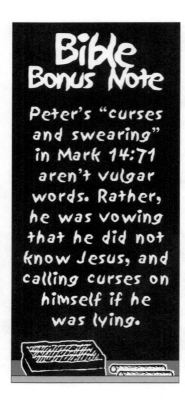

STEP 2 — MOVING UP

This step teaches students what a faithful friend looks like and that Jesus is always faithful to us.

Option 1 — Move It

You'll need Several Bibles, a white board and a dry-erase marker.

Ask students to list some qualities of a faithful friend (e.g., trustworthy, keeps secrets, dependable, honest, supportive, etc.) and write responses on the white board. Compile a fairly complete list; then explain: **We've considered what a faithful friend looks like, now let's check out how one of Jesus' best friends, Peter, treated Him.**

Ask for four volunteers and assign them the following roles to act out a brief drama: Jesus, Peter, the servant girl and the rooster. The rest of the group will act as extras and should be ready to participate when an action is called for that isn't fulfilled by one of the four roles already assigned (ad-libbing is encouraged!).

Read Mark 14:27-31,66-72, allowing time for roles to be acted out. When the drama is finished, incorporate the following biblical background into a discussion of the questions below.

- On the one hand, we can admire Peter because he wanted to stay geographically close to Jesus, yet he ended up betraying his friend.
- When Jesus warned the disciples that they would "fall away" in Mark 14:27, He didn't mean that they would lose their faith, but that they would momentarily lose their courage.
- When Jesus quoted Zechariah 13:7, one of the things He was showing was that His death was part of God's plan.
- esus knew for certain that Peter would be unfaithful, as evidenced by His phrase "I tell you the truth," as well as His conviction that it would happen that night.

What words come to mind to describe Peter's friendship with Jesus? Loyal, trustworthy, caring.

How many of these characteristics did Peter fulfill in this incident? At the time of his betrayal, none.

How would you respond if you were betrayed like Jesus was? Angry, hurt.

Ask the students who played the roles of Peter and Jesus to come forward and act out how they would respond if the same situation happened to them.

Distribute Bibles and ask for volunteers to read the following verses aloud: 1 John 3:16; 1 Corinthians 1:9 and 1 Thessalonians 5:24. Discuss:

What do these verses tell us about how God responds to us? He is faithful; He honors His word and His promises.

Do you think God responds that way when we act unfaithfully toward Him? Yes, regardless of how we act, His very nature prevents Him from being unfaithful.

What does this tell us about God? We might change, but He never will!

Option 2  Chat Room

You'll need Several Bibles, a white board, a dry-erase marker, a TV, a VCR and one of the following videos: *Rudy* or *The Sandlot*.

Ahead of time, decide which video you want to use for this option; then cue it as follows: cue *Rudy* approximately one hour and 33 minutes from the opening graphic to the scene depicting the coach's emotional reaction to the teammates' faithfulness to Rudy and their willingness to stick up for him; cue *The Sandlot* approximately 19 minutes from the opening graphic to the scene that shows one kid defending another who doesn't know anything about baseball.

Briefly discuss the following questions and write responses on the white board:

What does a faithful friend look like?

How does he or she act?

What kinds of things does he or she say?

Show the video clip and discuss whether or not the characters in the scene match any of the students' descriptions of a faithful friend. Divide students into four groups and erase the white board to make room to write the following information:

- Proverbs 17:17; 18:24; John 15:13; 1 John 3:16
- What's the main point of the verse?
- What is it asking us to do?
- What are the benefits to living out the verse?
- Why is it sometimes difficult to live out the verse?
- How was the verse illustrated in the video clip?
- In what ways have you seen the verse illustrated in life?
- How could you specifically apply this verse?

Instruct the groups to each choose two of the four verses to look up and have students apply and discuss all of the questions on the board to both verses.

Option 3  Pulse Points

You'll need Several Bibles, flash paper (available at most novelty or party supply stores), matches or a lighter and a fireproof receptacle in which to burn the paper.

The Big Idea
Jesus is a faithful friend.

The Big Question
What does a faithful friend look like?

1. A faithful friend is loyal.
Read Deuteronomy 31:6 and Matthew 28:20; then explain: **Faithful friends do the simple things, and they do them consistently because they care about their relationships with each other. God is the most loyal and faithful companion we can have—He has promised that no matter where we go, He will always be with us.**

2. A faithful friend is forgiving.
Read 1 John 1:9 and explain: **If we confess our sins, we can count on God's promise to forgive us, cleanse us from our sins and never leave us, because He is reliable.**

Hold up a piece of flash paper and burn it. Explain: **As quickly as this paper disappeared, God forgives our sins even quicker when we confess them to Him.**

3. A faithful friend is trustworthy.
Read 1 Corinthians 10:13 and remind students that just as God always provides help when we need it, we need to be trustworthy to our friends and support them when they need it.

Read aloud the story of Britain's Derek Redmond during the Barcelona Summer Olympics of 1992.

> **He was running the race of his life in the 400-meter semifinals and could see the finish line as he rounded the turn into the backstretch. Suddenly he felt a sharp pain go up the back of his leg. He fell face first onto the track with a torn hamstring.**

As the medical attendants were approaching, Redmond fought to his feet. He set out hopping, in a crazed attempt to finish the race. When he reached the stretch, a large man came out of the stands and embraced him. It was Jim Redmond, Derek's father. "You don't have to do this," he told his weeping son. "Yes, I do," said Derek. "Well, then," said Jim, "we're going to finish this together."

Derek didn't walk away with the gold medal, but he walked away with an incredible memory of a father who, when he saw his son in pain, left his seat in the stands to help him finish the race.

Jim Redmond modeled what any trustworthy, faithful friend would do.[1]

STEP 3
MOVING ON

This step helps students know that God will faithfully stay with them, and that they will never be separated from God's love.

Option 1  Chat Room

You'll need Several Bibles, copies of "He Loves Me, He Loves Me Not" (p. 62) and "How Do You Know?" (p. 63) and pens or pencils.

   Ahead of time (optional), prepare extra statistics by surveying people in a chat room of a popular website (get responses from Christians and non-Christians if possible) or survey people at your local supermarket or mall. You can even ask a few students to ask their parents to take the survey to work with them.

Divide students into groups of four to six. Distribute "He Loves Me, He Loves Me Not" and pens or pencils. Instruct students to fill out the surveys; then with the whole group, ask for volunteers to share their responses. Allow for group discussion; then distribute "How Do You Know?" Have students work together within their groups to complete the handout. Allow several minutes and then discuss their answers with the whole group.

Option 2  Real Life

You'll need Absotively nothing, but this book!

Read the journal entry below written by an eighth grader named Robert; then divide students into small groups to discuss the questions or conduct a whole-group discussion.

Monday

Today stunk. I hate school. I hate my friends. I hate my family. I hate my life. My dog is OK, but everything else stinks.

I can't stand the way Derek pretends to be my friend. As long as I save a seat for him at lunch or give him free movie passes from my dad's job or say nice things about him to Jessica, he's my friend. But those are the only times he cares about me.

My mom says she loves me, but she wouldn't buy that new shirt I wanted, and she never lets me stay out late. Everyone else's parents let them stay out late.

God, why are You letting all of this happen to me? Don't You care? I know You said You'd never leave me, but sometimes I wonder. If You love me, why do You let all this junk happen to me? Actually, *do* You even love me? Maybe You've forgotten about me. Is it because of that fight I got into with my dad? I'm so messed up. I want to say I hate You too, but that scares me.

Please help.

Discuss:

What would you say to Robert?

What would God say to him?

Have you ever felt like Robert feels? Everyone has at one time or another.

What did you do? (Students' answers will vary—be sure to validate those willing to share their experiences.)

Looking back, what do you wish you had done differently in that situation? Ah, the "looking back" question . . . everything seems so much clearer when you look back!

Option 3 Tough Questions

You'll need These questions and some students!

1. **Will God love me if I keep committing the same sin over and over?** The apostle Paul also had a terrible struggle with sin, even as a believer in Jesus (see Romans 7:7-26), yet God allowed him to see that "there is now no condemnation for those who are in Christ Jesus" (Romans 8:1). God's desire is to completely save us from our sins—that's why He sent Jesus (see John 3:16; Romans 5:8). If there are sins you have more trouble with than others, it means that you need *more* of God in your life, so that He can continue the process of making you more like Jesus (see 1 John 3:2).

Remember, too, that although it's painful to face the truth of sin in our lives, God is faithfully doing a good work in us and promises to be with us through the whole process.

2. **Does God love me even if I don't feel like loving Him back?** "God is love." This is stated in 1 John 4:8 and again in 4:16. What an amazing truth—that God not only loves, but that He actually *is* love. Our human capacity to feel love sometimes means that our ability to show that love is affected by our circumstances. God is always capable of loving us, even during times when we are not faithful in showing our love to Him.

3. **Why is it so important to be faithful to God and to my family and friends?** We'll just let Proverbs 3:3-6 speak for itself: "Let love and faithfulness never leave you; bind them around your neck, write them on the tablet of your heart. Then you will win favor and a good name in the sight of God and man. Trust in the LORD with all your heart and lean not on your own understanding; in all your ways acknowledge him, and he will make your paths straight."

4. **Do I have to be faithful to God even when things are going badly?** Yes! It's OK to be upset by circumstances and it's even OK to fail to understand how God could possibly use hard times to do something good, but you should always trust that, whether you understand it or not, God is faithful and He will do what's best (see Lamentations 3:22,23).

Job was a man who lost *everything* that was meaningful to him on earth; but his faith in God never came into question. He hurt because of what happened to him, but still he continued to praise and worship God. "Naked I came from my mother's womb, and naked I will depart. The LORD gave and the LORD has taken away; may the name of the LORD be praised" (Job 1:21,22). Powerful words from a faithful man.

STEP 4 MOVING OUT

This step reminds students that they have the choice to be a faithful Christian, friend and family member.

Option 1 Light the Fire

You'll need One legal-size envelope and a copy of "What I've Learned About Faithfulness" (p. 00) for every six to eight students and pens or pencils.

Ahead of time, create several sets of sentence strips by cutting the handouts apart and placing the strips into envelopes.

Divide students into groups of six to eight and distribute the envelopes. Explain: **One member at a time in each group is going to remove a strip of paper from the envelope; read it aloud and complete the sentence.** Let students know that they have the option of saying "skip" if they can't come up with an answer quickly and anyone who prefers not to complete a sentence can pass his or her turn altogether (but encourage everyone to participate and share what's on their hearts).

After everyone has shared (or had a chance to share) have groups close in prayer.

Option 2 Fired Up

You'll need A white board, a dry-erase marker, paper and pens or pencils.

Ask students to brainstorm at least 10 reasons why it's sometimes difficult to be faithful to God and others. Write responses on the white board; then divide students into groups of four to six and distribute paper and pens or pencils. Instruct groups to each choose five reasons from

the white board that they believe to be the most difficult; write them down and number them in order of difficulty (with 1 representing the most difficult and 5 the least).

Allow a couple of minutes for groups to write down their lists; then ask each group to share its top three. Have students share within their small groups how these difficulties might be overcome, making it possible to remain faithful to God and others. Invite group members to exchange names and phone numbers and to keep in touch during the upcoming week to encourage each other to remain faithful.

Have group members pray for one another by name; then finish in prayer with the whole group, thanking God for His endless faithfulness to us and asking Him to help students to remain faithful in their walks with Him.

Option 3 Spread the Fire

You'll need Jumbo-sized self-adhesive labels, felt-tip pens, paper and pens or pencils.

Explain: **Let's face it—we live in a slogan-filled society where we are bombarded with catchy phrases and cute artwork. Since society tends to communicate values through these areas, why not capitalize on it and use the same method to communicate God's values?!**

Divide students into small groups and have them brainstorm some practical slogans for faithfulness. Allow a few minutes for students to come up with ideas; then ask groups to share what they came up with as you write their ideas on the white board. Here's some ideas in case students get stuck: *Try Being Faithful! Try Faithfulness—You'll Like It! Friends Don't Let Friends Be Unfaithful! Want a Faithful Friend? BE a Faithful Friend!*

After writing responses on the white board, ask students to share some popular commercial slogans or art that reminds them of a particular product. After several slogans are shared, inform students that just as the slogans they heard remind them of certain products, so they too can create slogans and artwork that communicate applications of faithfulness.

Distribute labels and felt-tip pens and invite students to create their own bumper sticker using what they've learned in this session. Encourage them to place their stickers on a notebook or backpack—anywhere that someone might see them and take notice of their message.

Discuss:

How might Christians respond to your sticker?

What about non-Christians?

If a non-Christian asked you what it meant, what would you say? Have students practice responding to hypothetical non-Christian responses to make sure students are equipped for what might happen in school when someone asks them about their stickers; then close in prayer, thanking God for His everlasting faithfulness to His children and asking that He would give students boldness to use their faithfulness to show others about Jesus Christ.

Note

1. Taken from *Hot Illustrations for Youth Talks* by Wayne Rice. Copyright © 1995 by Youth Specialties, Inc. Used by permission of Zondervan Publishing House.

NOTES

He Loves Me, He Loves Me Not

Check your answer to each question and write out a response when necessary.

☐ Yes ☐ No Do you believe God exists?

☐ Yes ☐ No Do you believe God loves you?

If no, why not?

If yes, what could change that?

☐ Yes ☐ No Do you believe God would ever stop loving you?

If no, why?

If yes, under what condition?

What do you have to do in order for God to love you?

☐ Nothing

☐ Be good

☐ Go to church

☐ Other _____

How Do You Know?

Will God faithfully stay with you, no matter what?

"I give them eternal life, and they shall never perish; no one can snatch them out of my hand. My father, who has given them to me, is greater than all; no one can snatch them out of my Father's hand." John 10:28,29

According to this verse, how do you know God will stay with you?

Will God faithfully stay with you, no matter what?

"Therefore he is able to save completely those who come to God through him, because he always lives to intercede for them." Hebrews 7:25

According to this verse, how do you know He will stay with you, no matter what?

Will God faithfully stay with you, no matter what?

"For I am convinced that neither death nor life, neither angels nor demons, neither the present nor the future, nor any powers, neither height nor depth, nor anything else in all creation, will be able to separate us from the love of God that is in Christ Jesus our Lord." Romans 8:38,39

According to this verse, how do you know He will stay with you, no matter what?

What does this tell you about God?

If you were to take the "He Loves Me, He Loves Me Not" survey again, would your answers be different? Why or why not?

What I've Learned About Faithfulness

If I applied what I've learned about faithfulness, I could . . .

The biggest thing I've learned about faithfulness is . . .

If I could ask God any questions about faithfulness, I would ask Him . . .

If given the opportunity to share about faithfulness with someone, I would say . . .

One thing I think God wants me to do is . . .

One way others can pray for me is . . .

One way I can be a faithful friend is to . . .

One way I can be a faithful family member is to . . .

One way I can be a faithful Christian is to . . .

Devotions in Motion

WEEK FOUR: FAITHFULNESS

DAY 1

QUICK QUESTIONS

Find a clean spot in your room where you can read Joshua 24:14,15.

God Says

You can smell the aroma of freshly baked cookies as you walk through the door of your friend's house with her after school. Her mom offers you cookies fresh from the oven and a glass of cold, fresh milk. You wish your mom could be just like her, so you ask your friend if she can get you a picture of her mom. When you get home, you rush right into your room and tape the picture to your mirror.

Another friend invites you to go fishing with him and his dad on a Saturday. When you get back from fishing, you ask for a picture of your friend's dad, and it goes on the mirror with the other picture.

Before long you have a whole collection of pictures of other people's parents. You find yourself spending more time with your friend's parents than your own, and you even call them for advice instead of asking your own parents.

I Do

How is this story like, or unlike, your relationship with God?

Are there ways that you are ignoring your heavenly Father?

What two things can you do today to put more of a prior-ity on your relationship with God?

FOLD HERE ---

DAY 4

FAST FACTS

How's your reputation? Check out 3 John 3,4.

God Says

Jared tried to read his Bible every day for at least a few minutes. He never missed church on Sunday and he was active in the youth group. He especially enjoyed going with friends from church to clean up the local park and visit the senior cit-izens' home. Jared even got along with his family (at least most of the time).

At school, Jared had a spotless reputation. He didn't have problems like others kids, such as fights with friends or wild afterschool activities. It's not that Jared was so popular, but it seemed that no one could find a real reason not to like him.

I Do

When you are faithful to God, your whole life will reflect it. In fact, a great way to let others know you're a Christian is to show them how you live differently. Then answer their questions. Just continue to put one foot in front of the other in your walk with God, and your reputation will precede you.

If you know you need help in living as a Christian ask God in prayer to help you be more like Jesus.

FAST FACTS
Read Psalm 115:1 to discover where the glory goes.

God Says
"Hawaii, here we come!" Emilia heard her teammates shout as she scored the winning goal that would take her soccer team to the national championship. The team had been hoping, dreaming of a trip to the playoffs in Hawaii all season and now thanks to Emilia, their dream would be a reality.

She felt pleased too, but Emilia didn't gloat—in fact her teammates were surprised at how she played down the atten- tion. When they said, "It's all because of you, girl," she replied, "No, really it's all God. He blessed me with athletic talent, and I have been faithful to develop it over the years." Maybe they didn't get it, but Emilia knew who was really responsible for her mak- ing that goal and that it was Him who made it possible for her team to go to Hawaii.

I Do
Faithfulness to God means giving Him the credit rather than taking it for yourself. You do your part, and God does His. You practice, eat right, and play the game; God gave you your body, health and strength, and put you on the team.
Thank God for His faithfulness to you in allowing you to do all the things you do.

FOLD HERE

QUICK QUESTIONS
Read Psalm 117 and praise the Lord!

God Says
Imagine you have an on-again, off-again friend. Yesterday she was right by your side every chance she had. She wanted to know all your secrets and she confided her secrets to you. When you ate lunch with her, she implied that you'd spend your week- end together too.

Today she's buddied up to someone else and won't give you the time of day. You tried to ask about plans for Friday evening and she walked away arm-in-arm with her new best friend as if she didn't even hear you. Tomorrow she'll probably act like nothing happened and want to be friends again. How will you respond?

☐ "Hey, if I wasn't good enough for you yesterday, I'm prob- ably not good enough today, either."

☐ "Great to see you again!"

☐ "I'll never speak to you again!"

☐ "Are you sure you're my friend?"

I Do
Do you have an on-again, off-again friends? How do they make you feel?

Do you ever act that way yourself?

How faithfully are you in your relationship with God?

Choose a time of day and place to meet with God, and stick to it faithfully. I promise your friendship with God will only get better!

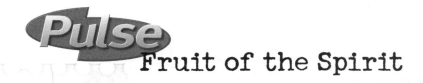

Fruit of the Spirit

The Big Idea

Real power is obtained through a gentle, Christlike nature.

Session Aims

In this session you will guide students to:

- Understand the true meaning of gentleness and how being gentle makes them powerful;
- Experience relief in knowing that they don't have to pretend to be someone they're not in order to appear tough;
- Choose to practice being gentle during their week.

The Biggest Verse

"Do you think I cannot call on my Father, and he will at once put at my disposal more than twelve legions of angels?" Matthew 26:53

Other Important Verses

Proverbs 15:1; 17:22; 25:15; Jeremiah 17:10; Matthew 26:47-56; Galatians 5:22,23; Colossians 3:12; 1 Peter 3:3,4

Gentleness

STEP

MOVING IN

This step shows students that being gentle is different than being weak.

Option 1  Move It

You'll need A bag of candy or a box of donuts for the winning team, 3x5-inch index cards and pens or pencils. **Note:** A few adult volunteers would be helpful during the game.

Welcome students and divide them into groups of four to six. Distribute index cards and pens or pencils and instruct students to write down a one-word definition of the word "gentle" on their index cards; then share their definitions within their groups. Allow a couple of minutes for sharing; then ask volunteers to share with the whole group what they wrote.

Stand in the middle of the room and invite one volunteer from each group to come forward to begin a game of Charades. Explain that there are four mammals (people or animals) that each group's volunteer will act out for the other group members. When a student in one small group gets the right answer he or she should run up to you, tell you the correct answer and then get the next clue, which you will whisper in his or her ear. Encourage students to try not to shout out their answers (yeah, right!) since that will give away the answer to other groups. First team to get all four words wins! Present the prize at the end of the meeting. The words are "Yoda," "Bill Gates," "Mother Teresa" and "a cheetah."

Discuss:

What's one word you could use to describe all of the people/animals in the game? Small, powerful, smart.

How is that different from the definition of "gentle" that you wrote on your card? Answers will vary depending on students' cards.

Explain: **Some people believe that being gentle means being weak, but gentleness has more to do with being powerful. None of the people/animals we acted out are physically large, but they are all powerful in some way. Today we're going to study how being gentle can be powerful.**

Option 2  Chat Room

You'll need A TV, a VCR and a video on the life of Dr. Martin Luther King, Jr. (PBS's *Eyes on the Prize* is a great one). You should be able to find one in your public library or video store.

Ahead of time, familiarize yourself with the content of the video and note specific areas of abuse that Dr. King suffered due to racism and prejudice (getting sprayed with fire hoses and attacked by dogs while marching, etc.) and clips of his reactions to that abuse: His consistently nonviolent responses and his speech "I Have a Dream" are good examples. Cue the video to the first scene you'll be showing.

Welcome students and let them know that you're going to show a video about Dr. Martin Luther King, Jr., but first you want to have a brief discussion on the topic of racism, prejudice and hatred. Discuss:

What is racism? Viewing someone in a certain way because of his or her race.

Where does it come from? Ignorance, fear, hatred, etc.

What are examples of racism in our world today? Our country? Our state? Our schools?

What are some ways you would respond to discrimination against yourself?

How have some people responded in the past? Wars, intimidation, gangs, turn the other cheek, etc.

Let's take a look at the life of Dr. Martin Luther King, Jr. and his radical approach to fighting the evils of racism. Show several minutes of footage featuring the abuse Dr. King and his fellow marchers suffered.

Discuss: **How do you think Dr. King should have responded to these acts against him?**

Show scenes demonstrating his consistent, nonviolent responses; include his "I Have A Dream" speech. Transition to the next step by explaining: **Dr. King's gentle, nonviolent approach was considered weak and ineffective by many—yet it was through his strength in spirit and his self-control that he changed American history. Dr. King made great advances toward freeing society of racism and discrimination. Today we're going to find out how God can use our gentleness to do great things.**

Option 3  Fun and Games

You'll need One die and candy for the winners. Some adult volunteers to help referee the game would also be recommended.

Welcome students and let them know that they're going to play Three (a combination of Musical Chairs, Red Rover and Red Light, Green Light). Designate a starting line and a finish line (you can do this indoors or out) and have stu-

dents line up behind the starting line. Choose one student to be the "All-Authoritative Destiny Maker" (AADM). Students will run back and forth from the starting line to the finish line while the AADM stands in the middle of the playing field, rolling the die and trying to come up with a three. When the AADM rolls a three, he should say, "Three!" Anyone caught between the start and finish lines when a three is rolled is out!

Continue until you only have one person remaining. Announce that you're going to award a prize to two winners—the one who crosses the most times successfully and the one left at the end of the game. Oh yeah: Determine how long a person can wait before making the mad dash (like 15 seconds); otherwise, a strategic thinker (or lazy person) will simply stand at the start line and wait until everyone else gets out. Time permitting, play a couple of rounds; then award candy prizes to the winners.

Transition to the next step by explaining: **When we think of a powerful person, we usually think of physical strength (such as a football player or body builder) or someone in a powerful position (such as the president of a country). In this game, though, the most powerful person was the one who didn't have to do a thing but roll a die. In fact, he could just have whispered when he rolled a three and we still would have to obey. Being gentle doesn't have anything to do with being weak—and right now we're going to take a look at how being gentle can actually mean being *powerful*.**

STEP 2 MOVING UP

This step helps students recognize that the word "gentle" means "power under control."

Option 1  Move It

You'll need Several Bibles, a variety of clothing items (from a thrift store; or have a real adventure and borrow clothes from a school's drama department), a white board and a dry-erase marker.

Ahead of time, prepare for Hangman by drawing

dashes on the white board to represent the phrase "Gentleness means power under control or quiet strength."

Ask two guys and two girls to come forward as team representatives—guys versus girls. Ask one of the guys to read Colossians 3:12 aloud; then ask one of the girls to read 1 Peter 3:3,4. Discuss:

Why do you think God mentions clothing and beauty in these verses? We often look to other things to make ourselves look good, but covering ourselves with gentleness is what's really meaningful and attractive.

What point are these verses conveying? Gentleness is much more important than we tend to think; it's what really makes us attractive to others.

God uses clothing and beauty to illustrate His truth in these passages, so right now we're going to search for the true meaning of the word "gentleness" with a variation of Hangman. Explain that instead of drawing stick figures and adding body parts when someone guesses the wrong letter, students will add articles of clothing to the four volunteers!

> **Note:** The phrase for the game is "Gentleness means power under control or quiet strength."

Explain these rules to students: **Designate one guy and one girl as the Dressers and the other guy and girl are the Dressees. Each team will take a turn guessing a letter. If a team guesses a letter correctly, you will write it in the correct blanks. If a team guesses *incorrectly*, the opposing team's Dresser will put an article of clothing on the Dressee for the incorrect team. By the end of the game, you should have two Dressees wearing an awful lot of clothing.** (Can you say "Great photo op"?!)

After the puzzle is solved, award lots of applause to the players; then divide students into small groups of three to five to discuss the phrase and what it means.

Allow several minutes; then distribute Bibles and ask groups to share what they think the phrase means. Ask a volunteer to read Matthew 26:47-56; then discuss:

Who is involved in the story? Jesus, Judas, the other disciples, an armed crowd of people.

What happens in the story?

How did Jesus show gentleness or power under control? Why is that important? He showed it by not hurting anyone—including the guards who came to arrest Him—even though He had the power to do so. This is important because He modeled what it means to be gentle even though He had the right to be angry.

Has there been a time in your life when you felt out-of-control and lost your temper? Were there any consequences?

Has there been a time in your life when you responded gently in a challenging situation? What happened as a result of your self-control?

Explain: **Jesus responded with gentleness, even though He could have completely destroyed His enemies. Right now we're going to take a look at ways we can respond with gentleness rather than anger and how it changes the results.**

Option 2  Chat Room

You'll need Several Bibles, a TV and VCR, and the video *Happy Gilmore*.

Ahead of time, cue the video approximately 22 minutes from the beginning to the two-minute scene in which Happy refuses to take advice on putting and then takes several swings before finally sinking the putt. Frustrated, Happy takes out his anger on a nearby observer.

> **Note:** This video is rated PG-13, which means you should pay extra attention to any objectionable language or content as you show these carefully selected scenes to students.

Begin a discussion by suggesting: **Let's take a look at one way a person chose to deal with a frustrating situation. Show the video;** then continue discussion:

What was going through Happy's mind while he was putting?

What other options did Happy have to deal with the situation?

Why do you think Happy chose the option he did?

Have you ever been in a situation where someone else's words drove you nuts? How did you respond?

Was your response effective? Why or why not?

Explain: **Happy Gilmore used his power on someone else. He couldn't control himself, and his lack of self-control hurt someone else. Let's see how Jesus responded to a similar situation.** Read Matthew 26:47-56; then discuss:

What might have been going through Jesus' mind as the crowd approached Him armed with swords and clubs? A realization that this was His time to die for our sins, apprehension about what was going to happen, concern for the safety of His disciples, confidence in who God is.

How do you think Judas's betrayal affected Jesus? Jesus knew that Judas would betray Him, but that doesn't mean that He wasn't affected by it. He probably felt saddened by the betrayal of His trusted friend.

What other options did Jesus have in order to deal with that situation? To fight back physically, to call on God's army of angels to protect Him, to disappear, to verbally criticize his accusers.

Why did Jesus choose the option He did? He wanted to model what it meant to be gentle, even when He had the right to act otherwise. He was also following God's plan.

Explain: **Jesus responded with gentleness, even though He could've completely destroyed His enemies. Let's take a look at some ways we can respond with gentleness instead of anger and how it changes the results.**

Option 3 Pulse Points

You'll need Several Bibles, a hammer and a rock.

The Big Idea
God has provided a way for us to live powerful lives.

The Big Question
What is a powerful life in God's eyes?

1. Get the right clothes.
Distribute Bibles and ask for a volunteer to read Colossians 3:12. Discuss the word "clothe" and what it means in today's world. Explain: **Worldly fashions are constantly changing, but clothing ourselves in compassion, kindness, humility, gentleness and patience will always look good!**

2. Examine your heart.
Read 1 Peter 3:3,4. Ask for a volunteer to help you demonstrate a game that tests reflexes. Place your hands out (palms up), while your partner rests his hands on top of yours (palms down). The goal is for him to move his hand before you slap it. If he's too quick and you miss; reverse roles and try to avoid his slap! Invite students to play the game with the person next to them, reminding them to play *gently*.

Allow a moment for students to play; then explain: **Just like getting your hand slapped leaves a mark, we leave a mark on others' lives when we act selfishly and focus more on ourselves than others. Just as you tried to avoid getting your hand slapped in this game, so will others begin to avoid the marks your uncaring ways or negative attitudes leave on them.**

3. Never speak too quickly.
Read Proverbs 25:15; then try to break the rock with the hammer. Explain: **As powerful as this hammer is, it can't**

break this rock. Yet, our words are so powerful that a gentle word can make a huge mark on another person's life—and so can a harsh one.

4. Talk to God.

Read Proverbs 15:1; then share a story from your own life about a time when a gentle word turned away anger and a harsh word stirred it up.

5. Learn to laugh at yourself.

Read Proverbs 17:22; then share another personal story that shows the value of humor and the importance of not taking ourselves so seriously.

6. Evaluate where God is in your life.

Read Jeremiah 17:10 and ask students to reflect on whether they've been trying to live a powerful life in the world's way or God's way. Remind them that when they combine compassion, kindness, humility, gentleness and patience, they will live a powerful life.

STEP **3**
MOVING ON

This step shows students how being gentle can make a difference in their lives and in the lives of others.

Option 1 — Chat Room

You'll need One copy of "What Would Happen If . . ." (p. 75) for every four to six students.

Divide students into groups of four to six and distribute "What Would Happen If . . ." Allow a few minutes for groups to discuss the scenarios; then instruct each group to select one of the scenarios and prepare a short skit based on the previous discussion. Have groups perform their skits one at a time. After each skit, ask audience members to yell out what the skit says about gentleness.

Option 2 — Real Life

You'll need Four copies of "I Feel Like a Wimp!" (p. 76).

Ask for three volunteers to act out an impromptu drama. Assign each volunteer a role from "I Feel Like a Wimp!" and distribute a copy to each actor. Have actors present the drama. When the thunderous applause dies down, discuss:

What are some ways Lewis could respond to the situation?

What are the potential consequences of each option?

What are the potential benefits of each option?

What would *you* do?

What should Lewis do?

Option 3 — Tough Questions

You'll need Several Bibles and these questions.

Distribute a Bible to anyone who doesn't have one; then discuss:

1. **How can I be gentle when others continually make fun of me?** The easy thing would be to simply respond the same way they treat you. But Proverbs 15:1 explains why being gentle is the right response, even though it can be tough—because it turns away wrath.

2. **Why is it so hard to be gentle toward certain people?** Because certain people rub us the wrong way! But no matter what, Galatians 5:22,23 shows us how we need to live to show God's control of our lives: by being loving, patient, kind, good, faithful, gentle and full of self-control.

3. **What if I'm trying to be gentle and loving toward someone, but I really can't stand the person?** First of all, you're doing the right thing by trying to be gentle and loving—but you won't be able to continue to do this without God's help. You should continue to

pray that God will change your heart toward the person and ask Him to show you the person through His eyes. Ask for wisdom to deal with this person in gentleness.

4. **Jesus had the power to destroy His enemies. Why didn't He?** In Matthew 26:47-56, Jesus made it clear that He could've wiped everyone out but that He was more concerned with doing what His Father wanted Him to do than He was about protecting Himself.

5. **Does being gentle ever work?** There are *tons* of examples of the power of gentleness. People like Martin Luther King, Jr., and Mother Teresa made a huge impact because they handled difficult situations with nonviolence by caring for others more than themselves and living as examples of God's gentleness.

STEP 4
MOVING OUT

This step reminds students that a commitment to respond gently in situations is a reflection of the powerful life of Christ.

Option 1
Light the Fire

You'll need Several gift Bibles and a couple of friends to practice the skit on just in case students get stuck!

Ask for three quick-thinking, brave volunteers to act out an impromptu skit called "Three Gentle Men." Here's how the skit plays out: The audience will name a location (lunchroom, movie theater, party, etc.) and Volunteer One will begin describing the wonders of this place and all that's happening there. After a few seconds, the audience will name a conflict (an argument broke out, the lights went off, someone tripped while carrying her lunch tray, etc.) and Volunteer Two will develop the conflict in the setting described by Volunteer One. Finally (patience now, we're getting there), Volunteer Three will wrap it all up by applying gentleness to the situation described by Volunteers One and Two!

After the first attempt, ask volunteers to switch roles and try again. If you have enough time, you can give three new volunteers the opportunity to try it, too.

Explain: **Think of a situation during the past week where you had the opportunity to respond with gentleness. Did you demonstrate gentleness? If not, how could you have responded differently?** Allow time for students to think about this. Announce that there will be a time of silent prayer. Those who are already Christians will use the time to silently pray, asking God to give them the strength to respond to challenging situations during the next week with gentleness. Continue: **If you're not a Christian, I want you to know that God loves you and wants to be Lord of your life. During this silent time, open your heart to God and share it with Him. Thank Jesus for dying on the cross for your sins and invite Him to become number one in your life.**

Allow several minutes of quiet prayer; then invite those who asked Jesus into their lives to come and see you after the meeting so that you can give them a gift Bible and welcome them into the family of God!

Option 2 — Fired Up

You'll need A white board, a dry-erase marker, paper, the Sunday comics and colored pens or pencils.

Write the words of Proverbs 15:1 on the white board and divide students into small groups. Distribute paper and colored pens or pencils to each group; then explain: **We're going to conclude this session on gentleness by illustrating how Proverbs 15:1 is true in each of our lives. Think back to a time recently when you argued or had difficulty with someone and draw a two- or three-paneled cartoon strip of what that argument was about.**

Allow several minutes for students to complete their cartoons; then ask a few volunteers to share what they've drawn. Now instruct students to re-create the same scene, adding what might have happened if they had responded with gentleness during the argument (specific words, body actions, etc.).

If time permits, have students share their drawings, and point out that the first group of pictures demonstrates the second half of Proverbs 15:1, and the second group demonstrates the first half of that verse. Close in prayer, thanking God for His gentleness and asking Him to help students follow His example by choosing to live in the way their second drawings depict.

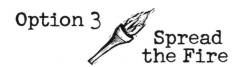

Option 3 — Spread the Fire

You'll need Index cards and pens or pencils.

Explain: **Jesus lived a powerful life—demonstrating His power through gentleness.** Distribute index cards and pens or pencils and instruct students to follow each direction below as you read it aloud:

- **Write down the initials of five people who are picked on or ignored at your school.**
- **Circle the initials of the three you see most often at school.**
- **Take a moment to consider how your actions might help these three people to grow closer to God; then write down two ways that you can show the powerful love of Christ this week to each of the three people you identified.**

Close in prayer, asking God to give students the opportunity to show Christ's love this week to the people in their lives. Let students know that you will be asking them next week to find out what happened when they showed gentleness to the people they wrote down (and be sure to follow through next week).

NOTES

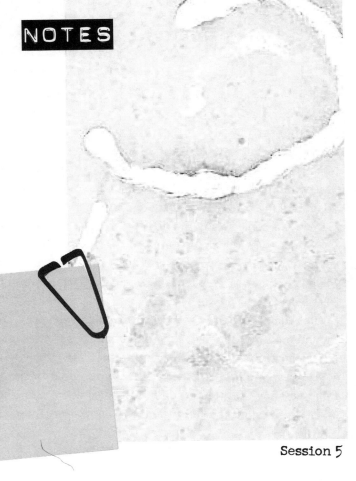

What Would Happen If . . .

- YOU FOCUSED ON THE POSITIVE QUALITIES OF THE PERSON WHO ANNOYS YOU?

- YOU RESPONDED WITH A COMPLIMENT EVERY TIME SOMEONE OFFENDED YOU?

- YOU TOOK TIME TO THINK ABOUT WHAT YOU WERE GOING TO SAY BEFORE RESPONDING IN A HEATED CONVERSATION?

- YOU PRAYED TO God FOR HELP ANYTIME THAT YOU WERE IN A TOUGH SITUATION?

- YOU REGULARLY PRAYED FOR THOSE PEOPLE WHO BOTHER YOU?

- YOU DID SOMETHING NICE FOR A PERSON OTHERS PICK ON?

- YOU ALWAYS SAVED A SEAT AT LUNCH FOR THE LONER AT SCHOOL?

- YOU HAD THE POWER TO CHANGE ONE THING ABOUT YOURSELF THAT YOU DIDN'T LIKE?

- YOU HAD A CHOICE BETWEEN BEING POPULAR BUT NOT FEELING GOOD ABOUT YOURSELF, OR NOT BEING POPULAR BUT FEELING GOOD ABOUT YOURSELF?

- YOU HAD THE REPUTATION OF LIVING LIKE JESUS?

I Feel Like a Wimp!

Cast

Jenny

Lewis

Gerard

Barbara

Jenny: Lewis, why are you acting like this? I've never seen you like this before!

Lewis: *(Obviously angry and upset.)* I just can't stand Gerard. He always puts me down in front of you and everyone else--and I hate it!

Jenny: Well, why don't you do something about it?

Lewis: What am I supposed to do, hit him or something?

Jenny: Duh, well, why not? Unless you stick up for yourself, he's just going to keep bugging you.

Lewis: I feel like such a wimp! I want to hit him so badly! But that makes me feel guilty, like God is talking to me or something.

Jenny: I know you're into Jesus and stuff, but not hitting him does sound kind of wimpy to me too. Wait. Here he comes.

Gerard: Hey look, it's the wimp.

Barbara: Come on, Gerard, give him a break.

Gerard: What for? He's got nothing going for him. I mean, look who he's hanging out with. Jenny is such a loser.

Barbara: Hey, that's not right.

Jenny: Lewis, are you going to do something?

Gerard: Yeah, wimp. Aren't you going to do something?

Devotions in Motion

Week Five: Gentleness

DAY 1

Quick Questions

Learn how to speak from Proverbs 15:1.

God Says

Your best friend accuses you of telling people at school that he likes a certain girl. The thing is, you know that it's not true that he likes her (at least not for more than a friend) and you wouldn't have told anyone even if it were—but he's really mad and won't listen to you. You respond to his ranting and raving by . . .

- ☐ Getting mad and yelling back.
- ☐ Smiling and saying "I'm sorry you think I hurt you."
- ☐ Walking away quietly.
- ☐ Telling everyone about the girl you know he does like.

I Do

How do you respond when someone gets mad at you—do you yell back or do you respond with gentleness? What about when you're wrongly accused—don't you want to defend yourself?

Do you find yourself thinking about the situation staying angry even after it's over?

How could responding with gentleness make the situation better?

The next time you get angry, try holding your breath while you count to 10 and pray; then respond with gentleness.

FOLD HERE -

DAY 4

Fast Facts

Before you get dressed, read Colossians 3:12.

God Says

Tanya always had the best clothes. She saved her allowance until she had enough to buy a few nice, stylish items at a time. Her accessories were simple but matched perfectly. Tanya didn't have a lot of money, but you wouldn't know it to look at her. Her closet would be the envy of all of her friends—if she had many.

Unfortunately for her, Tanya didn't have a lot of friends. She didn't listen very closely while others talked and she was quick to jump in with stories about herself before people were done talking. She rarely returned phone calls or kept appointments. She never apologized, even when she knew she was at fault, yet she had little patience for those who wouldn't apologize to her.

I Do

What you wear on your body makes little difference if you haven't carefully dressed your character. Great clothes only impress people for a short amount of time, if at all. It's your character and the way you treat others that will cause people to respect you and want relationships with you.

Pray that God will help you work more on what's on the inside of you than the outside.

FAST FACTS

Stressed out? Read Matthew 11:29 to find rest.

God Says

Derek had the third highest grade point average in his school. He served on the student council and played on the baseball team. At church, he led the activities team for his youth group leadership committee and sang in the choir. He had little time for friends and just hanging out. Derek had too much going on.

At a church retreat, Derek heard that Jesus wanted to give him rest. Derek laughed. Jesus wanted him to do his best, right? That's just what he thought he was doing. But by the end of the weekend, Derek knew that Jesus was gently asking him to trust Him rather than trusting in himself through life.

Derek's still a busy guy, but he's made time to relax, and he lets others lead the way . . . well, at least some of the time.

I Do

Learning from Jesus means making changes in your life. Society tells you to be aggressive, to do everything you're good at and with gusto. Jesus tells you to do your best, but to do everything with gentleness and a humble heart. You don't have to do it all. You can rest in Jesus' gentle arms.

What are two ways you can rest in Jesus this week?

FOLD HERE

QUICK QUESTIONS

Gently pick up your Bible and read Philippians 4:5.

God Says

Imagine Jesus always standing next to you. Does knowing He is near you change your response to any of the following situations?

- You encounter a stray dog while walking home from school.
- A person who looks homeless asks you for some change outside the mall.
- A friend asks if you'll go with her to talk to a teacher. Even though she's nervous about it, you'd prefer to grab a soda with your buddies.
- Your dad asks you to mow the lawn.
- Your little sister asks to tag along with you and your friends to the movies Saturday night.

I Do

If you could see Jesus with you, would you be more gentle or would you respond in the same way? Why?

Why do you think Jesus wants you to be gentle?

Is there someone (or a group of people) with whom you have a hard time being gentle? What is one thing you can do about it this week?

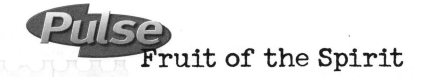
Fruit of the Spirit

The Big Idea

God is always patient with us, and we should be patient with each other.

Session Aims

In this session you will guide students to:

- Understand that God is patient and doesn't give up on them;
- Experience the peace that comes from knowing God has their best interests in mind;
- Develop a plan that will help them focus on God and not on their situations this week.

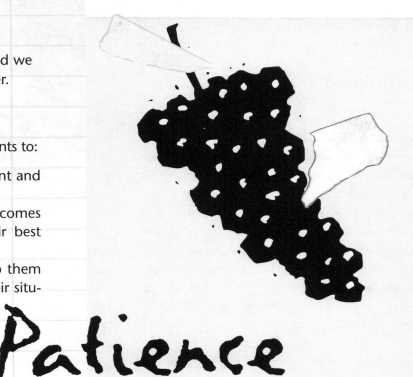

Patience

The Biggest Verse

"The third time he said to him, 'Simon son of John, do you love me?' " John 21:17

Other Important Verses

Psalm 40:1; Lamentations 3:25; Joel 2:12,13; Matthew 5:38-47; 18:21,22; John 21:15-19; Romans 8:38,39; 12:20,21; Philippians 1:6; Colossians 3:12,13; James 1:2-4; 2 Peter 3:9

STEP 1
MOVING IN

This step reminds students that they need patience in order to understand what God is doing in their lives.

Option 1 — Move It

You'll need Paper, a felt-tip pen, transparent tape, several easy-to-assemble children's puzzles (exact number depends on the size of your group), each with the same number of pieces and tables, equal in number to the amount of puzzles you have.

Ahead of time, use the paper and felt-tip pen to create number signs to designate each team's tables.

Also ahead of time, set up the tables at one end of the room (one table per puzzle) and tape the number signs to the front. **Option:** If you don't have enough tables, floor space marked off with masking tape will do.

Welcome students and divide them into as many teams as you have puzzles for. Assign each team a number and point out the tables corresponding to each number. Instruct teams to line up single file, one behind the other, at the opposite end of the room from the tables and give each person one piece from his or her team's puzzle.

Here's how to play: At your signal, the first person in each team will race to his team's table and place his puzzle piece in the middle; then race back to his team and tag the next player, who will run to the table and attempt to put the two puzzle pieces together (if they fit!). The relay will continue until one of the teams completes its puzzle and wins the game.

Start the game and after you've awarded the winning team with applause, discuss:

How many of you knew what your team's puzzle picture would be, based on your one puzzle piece?

At what point did you know what the finished picture would be?

Transition to the next step by explaining: **Just as you had to patiently wait before discovering what the pictures on your puzzles looked like, so it is with how God sometimes works in our lives. Sometimes we simply**

have to wait to find out what God is doing with all of the things happening around us and to us that we can't seem to understand. As we're going to see today, it's not always easy, but patience always pays off when we're patient with God.

Option 2 — Chat Room

You'll need A TV, a VCR and the video *Rudy.*

Ahead of time, cue the video approximately an hour and 39 minutes from the opening graphic to the scene in which Rudy gets a chance to do what he has always wanted—play in a Notre Dame football game.

Welcome students and after everyone is seated, discuss:

What value is there in waiting for something that you really want? It can make you appreciate it even more.

What makes waiting for something you really want difficult? Wanting something right away, wanting satisfaction right now, being afraid you won't get it.

Have you ever had to wait for something and had to wait longer than you thought you should have? We all have! Ask for a few examples.

Explain: **Let's take a look at someone who wanted something for as long as he could remember—and what he had to deal with while he waited for it to happen.**

Show the video clip; then discuss:

How did Rudy respond when he finally got in the game? He was happy and proud.

What do you think he learned by waiting as long as he did? He learned patience and perseverance. He also learned a great deal from those around him while he was waiting, so he gained maturity too.

Think back to a time that you had to wait for something. What did you learn during that process?

Is there anything in life you're waiting for now? Isn't there always?!

Transition to the next step by explaining: **Just as Rudy had to wait to play football, there are things in life that we have to wait for. But when God has us wait for something, we can be sure His timing is always perfect—even during times when it might not feel that way. Today we're going to check out what the Bible has to say about trusting God's perfect timing.**